Creative Lighting
for
OUTDOOR LIVING

Creative Lighting
for
OUTDOOR LIVING

40 FESTIVE PROJECTS

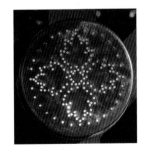

CHRIS RANKIN

LARK BOOKS
A Division of Sterling Publishing Co., Inc.
New York

Editors: Deborah Morgenthal,
Joanne O'Sullivan, Terry Taylor
Art Director: Dana Irwin
Layout and Production: Tom Metcalf
Photography: Evan Bracken
Production Assistance: Hannes Charen
Assistant Editor: Veronika Alice Gunter
Proofreader: Kim Catanzarite

Library of Congress Cataloging -in- Publication Data

Rankin, Chris
    Creative lighting for outdoor living: 40 festive projects / Chris Rankin.
        p. cm.
    Includes index
    ISBN 1-57990-213-8
    1. Exterior lighting. 2. Entertaining. 3. Landscape gardening. I. Title.

TK4188.R36 2001
747'.92–dc21

                                                    CIP
                                            00-053472

    10 9 8 7 6 5 4 3 2 1

Published by Lark Books, a division of
Sterling Publishing Co., Inc.
387 Park Avenue South, New York, N.Y. 10016

© 2001, Lark Books

Distributed in Canada by Sterling Publishing,
c/o Canadian Manda Group, One Atlantic Ave., Suite 105
Toronto, Ontario, Canada M6K 3E7

Distributed in the U.K. by Guild of Master Craftsman Publications Ltd., Castle Place,
166 High Street, Lewes, East Sussex, England
BN7 1XU
Tel: (+ 44) 1273 477374, Fax: (+ 44) 1273 478606, Email:
pubs@thegmcgroup.com, Web: www.gmcpublications.com

Distributed in Australia by Capricorn Link (Australia) Pty Ltd., P.O.
Box 6651, Baulkham Hills, Business Centre
NSW 2153, Australia

The written instructions, photographs, designs, patterns, and projects in this volume are
intended for the personal use of the reader and may be reproduced for that purpose
only. Any other use, especially commercial use, is forbidden under law without written
permission of the copyright holder.

Every effort has been made to ensure that all the information in this book is accurate.
However, due to differing conditions, tools, and individual skills, the publisher cannot be
responsible for any injuries, losses, and other damages that may result from the use of
the information in this book.

If you have questions or comments about this book, please contact:
Lark Books
50 College St.
Asheville, NC 28801
(828) 253-0467

Printed in Hong Kong

ISBN 1-57990-213-8

Table of Contents

Introduction

Whether you grew up in the country, city, or suburbs, you probably have fond childhood memories of long summer days that melted gently into evening, and the special feeling that came from being outside just as the sun dipped below the horizon. Twilight was a magical time, the last chance to squeeze in a few more moments in the fading light, playing tag or capture the flag, relishing your time outdoors before being called in to dinner and inevitably to bed. As adults we still feel the same longing at dusk. We want to stay outside a little while longer, experiencing the warmth and beauty of the outdoors, enjoying the fruits of our labor in the garden, or just soaking in the ambience of the night. Fading light doesn't have to signal the end of your enjoyment. The right lighting can help you extend your time outdoors well into the evening.

In the past, outdoor lighting was all about purpose, with little attention paid to style. Nowadays, an outdoor lighting plan can be both practical and beautiful. Lighting can enhance the

With a full moon rising above, you only need a few simple candles on your outdoor table to create enough glow for an enchanting evening under the stars.

design elements of your home, help you enjoy your time outdoors, and improve the security of your property. But the real value of lighting is more elusive. It's the way it transforms our mood, stimulates our senses, and changes our perspective, both literally and figuratively. Lighting accentuates the most beautiful elements in our surroundings, creating a palette of light and shadows on the blank canvas of night. With a little creative flare, outdoor lighting can lift our spirits and illuminate our nights.

This book will provide you with inspiring ideas for adding light to your garden, porch, deck, or backyard. The focus is on easy-to-make ways to create ambient and accent lighting for your outdoor spaces and activities. Whether you're seeking a way to highlight some of your horticultural gems, planning an evening get-together on the patio, or just looking for a little illumination for that dark corner on your deck, you'll find a project to suit your needs.

Most of the lighting techniques in this book are low-tech, temporary, and adaptable, giving you the flexibility you need to adjust your lighting for different areas and different situations. If you decide to make permanent outdoor electrical lighting part of your plan, you can buy a low-voltage lighting kit to install yourself, or hire a lighting consultant or electrician to help you design and install a more detailed approach to lighting.

Although nothing can match the luminous glow of the moon or the iridescent sparkle of a star-filled sky, these simple and innovative outdoor lighting projects are guaranteed to enhance the time you spend in your outdoor rooms.

A bridge lined with lit torches beckons you to discover what lies beyond your sight.

Oil lamps have been used to light the night for centuries, and are still an attractive and functional option today.

THE RIGHT LIGHT:
Creating an Outdoor Lighting Plan

Daylight doesn't play favorites—the sun illuminates all your outdoor features equally. But at night, you've got a chance to call the shots. You can lavish attention on your new outdoor sculpture, but keep your garbage cans covered in darkness. With a flexible lighting plan, you can change lighting to suit your shifting taste and moods, adding and taking away light as you wish.

Whether your needs call for temporary or permanent lighting, the following steps will help you to develop a plan that works for you.

Subtle downlights mounted on a trellis and fixed with shields focus light on this deck.

1. Consider the function your lighting will serve. Do you want to improve the view from inside your home or set the stage for guests who will be approaching your house for a party? Are you planning an intimate meal outdoors or are you trying to display your new garden sculpture? Will you be working late in the garden or just reading a book on the patio in the fading light?

2. Draw a sketch of your property and its features. What are the highlights of your outdoor space and what do you want to showcase? Take stock of all your outdoor elements: steps, pathways, pools, fences, decks, plantings, and outdoor art. Consider which garden elements are now leafy or flowering, and how they will change over time. Keep in mind that you're creating dark areas, too—what do you want to hide?

3. Look at your property in terms of focal points and lines of sight—what do you want to light and what angle will you be looking at it from? If you're lighting for a party, where will you and your guests be positioned—mingling on the patio or sitting at an elegantly appointed table? How close are your neighbors and how will your light affect them? Think about which way shadows will fall.

4. Decide on the strength and intensity of light you need. If you'll be working in your garden or cooking after dark, you'll need a stronger light

than you will for decorative effects. Do you want a warm glow or a focused beam?

5. Consider the time frame of your lighting plan. Do you need lighting outdoors for a few hours, for one night, or for every night? If you'll be using temporary electrical lighting, think about your outlets and reliance on extension cords—where will you plug in the cords? Remember, too, that overuse of cords becomes unsightly and dangerous. Consider using candles or torches in areas that can't be reached with cords—just make sure they are steadily mounted, and have a back up plan in case Mother Nature gives you a windy evening.

If you want to add permanent electrical fixtures, consider buying a kit at a home improvement center or consulting a lighting expert. Before committing to a permanent plan, experiment using clip-on lights mounted on garden stakes.

6. Finally, you'll need to chose your fixtures. Decide whether they will be hidden or seen.

Do you want fixtures that complement the architectural style of your house? From bronze, brass, and copper, to granite or cement, you can find fixtures in any style at home and garden centers—or better still, make your own using the ideas in this book.

Once you've decided what to light, see our techniques section for tips on how to achieve the effect you're looking for.

Lights directed downward amongst low-lying plants will spread pools of light around a general area.

A combination of electric light and candlelight allows you to achieve a variety of effects.

SPECIAL EFFECTS:
Creative Lighting Techniques

When lighting our homes and property at night, we try re-create the best of what we see in nature. Like the sun, electric lights and candles cast shadows. Like the moon and stars, they create a glow. During the day, the sun is in charge, deciding what to light and what to leave in shadow. At night, you can be the boss. The key to a successful outdoor lighting plan is to find the right light source, in the right place, focused on the right feature.

Are you feeling artistic? You can paint or sculpt with light—filling in light where you want it on your property, and taking away where you don't. Feeling cramped? You can open up space with the right lighting technique. Looking for more safety and security? Lighting can illuminate your home and garden to discourage intruders and help you find your way in the dark. Want to create a night to remember? Imaginative lighting can impress your guests and set the mood.

The techniques listed below are generally associated with electrical lighting, but you can adapt them for use with other lighting sources as well. Experiment to find out what works for you.

Paths and plantings are highlighted with different techniques that are both functional and aesthetically pleasing.

Tiny light bulbs recessed under a railing illuminate steps and create a lighted boundary between outdoor rooms and open space.

Uplighting: Lighting from the Ground Up

While the sun is out, everything is lit from above. Nightfall gives you the opportunity to see outdoor features from a different perspective. *Uplighting* describes the technique of illuminating from the underside—the opposite of natural daylight. Lighting fixtures can be placed on the ground or buried, set under plants and trees, or placed underwater in a pond or pool to shine upward and away from the viewer. This effect creates a soft glow that highlights the sculptural quality of trees or bushes and other objects. Uplighting looks great with tall trees and plants, such as firs or cypress, water features, sculpture, and other yard art.

Downlighting: Imitation Moonlight

Also called *moonlighting*, the technique of *downlighting* replicates natural moonlight, shining light down from a tree or high post to make it look as if the moon had chosen to rest in the upper branches of your tree alone. This technique creates a soft light which casts interesting shadows. Moonlighting is particularly flattering for trees, but also lights pathways effectively. When mounting fixtures to downlight a feature, don't place them too high up or it will be quite challenging to change the bulbs.

Spotlighting: A Star Is Born

Borrowing a technique from theater, *spotlighting* involves lighting a specific architectural feature or plant with an overhead mounted fixture. A good shield is essential to prevent glare from a spotlight. You'll want to use this technique sparingly—too many spotlights can make your yard look like a circus ring. Choose only your best features for this kind of lighting, or use it to light entryways and protect your home from intruders. Spotlighting can be a good way to light an outdoor cooking area.

Grazing: Painting with Light

Grazing allows you to paint with light—your fixtures become your brush and your techniques are your brushstrokes. To graze light on a feature,

Recessed lighting adds an unexpected and sophisticated element to this patio.

Lights graze this wall, showing off the texture. Mounted lights on top of the wall illuminate trees from the underside.

Shielded downlights cast enough light to walk in safety, but don't cause glare or overwhelm the landscape.

position the light source close to a wall and pointed slightly upward. The light will skim the surface, accentuating textured areas, dappling the wall with light and shadows. Grazing is a good choice if you have stucco or elaborate brickwork on your house, or low-lying plants with interesting textures, such as ornamental grasses. You may want to graze light in your garden even if don't have a particular plant you want to feature—the effect highlights the overall texture of your plantings.

Floodlighting: Pools of Light

For large, flat expanses of grass and areas with few plantings, *floodlighting* is a good way to provide general illumination and security. The effect, which looks like a "pool of light," is achieved by using a broad beam placed at a fairly high level. Floodlighting is not effective with a small garden—it will only accentuate the small size. If you use this technique, be mindful of light trespass—you don't want to floodlight your neighbor's property.

Path Lighting or Tasklighting: Leading You Down the Garden Path

Just as the name suggests, the technique *of path lighting* has a practical application—helping you see your way. Path lights are usually placed low to the ground and pointed downward so the light spills around a large area. Anti-glare shields are especially important for path lights, as glare could cause a misstep. Path lights can also be recessed in the ground and fitted with filters to diffuse the light.

Glaring Mistakes: Avoiding Outdoor Lighting Pitfalls

Creating an outdoor lighting scheme requires careful planning. Successful design will seem natural and effortless, but design flaws will have an obvious impact. The lighting may be too bright or not bright enough. Your party guests may be squinting from glare, or your house may be lit up like a prison yard. Achieving beauty and comfort is your goal. Here is a list of lighting pitfalls and some tips on how to avoid them.

Glare

Direct lighting in the eyes can damage not only the mood of a party, but also the eye tissue of the viewer. Glare usually occurs when a fixture lights from the side instead of from above or below. The light catches the eye and can cause discomfort and temporary vision loss. Placing light directly at eye level will also cause glare. To avoid glare, fit your fixtures with shields that direct and focus the light, and prevent it from being "wasted" in areas where you don't want it.

Overlighting

With outdoor lighting the old adage "less is more" often applies. Brighter is not necessarily better. The more brightly an area or object is lit, the darker the shadows will fall around it. Aesthetically, brighter lights are not as pleasing—they're reminiscent of institutional lighting used for parking lots and stadiums. Using a greater number of fixtures with less powerful lights will achieve a well-lit look without over powering the scenery.

Consider also the brightness of the light coming out of your house. When your indoor lighting is too bright, it can overwhelm your outdoor lighting scheme and cause what is known as the "black mirror effect"—erasing your view and leaving you with nothing to look at but the darkness outside.

Remember, lighting is like any accessory—overdoing it throws off the balance of the design and diminishes its appeal.

Light Trespass

A loud stereo blasting from the house next door can be a nuisance. A bright floodlight glaring in your window can have the same effect. Mounting a light too high up a tree can shoot the light straight past your property and right into the neighbor's yard, giving them unwanted illumination. When planning your lighting, make sure you know where it will fall. Stand away from your own property and check the scope of the light to make sure it is not bothering others.

Electrical and Fire Hazards

While the lighting techniques used in this book are simple, remember you are dealing with electricity and flame, and there are potential dangers. An extension cord from your home isn't designed to be used outside—make sure your outdoor extension cords are waterproofed: wet cords cause electrical shock. Your outdoor outlets should be weather-proofed as well. When using candles, keep flames away from anything that could catch fire. If children or pets are around, place all candles out of their reach. Keep an eye on your candles as they burn lower—the flame should be out before the candle reaches the candleholder. Your lanterns or candleholders should be placed on a steady surface. On windy nights, watch candles carefully to make sure they don't tip over.

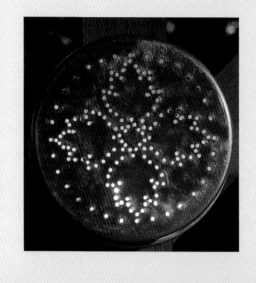

Creative Lighting Projects

F rom playful to sophisticated, fun to functional, you'll find a project here to light your outdoor space, enhance your landscape design, and create the right ambience for your evening under the stars.

Hot Peppers Candelabra

Designer
Chris Rankin

Impress your guests with the bounty of your summer garden by creating a candelabra using bright bell peppers. If you don't let the candles completely burn down, you can chop up the peppers to use in your next salsa, or make a savory family meal of stuffed peppers the next evening.

What You Need

5 or 6 bell peppers

Platter or flat basket

Candle adhesive (optional)

Large nail, diameter equal to or slightly smaller than the tapers

Thin beeswax tapers

Sharp kitchen knife (optional)

What You Do

1
Condition your beeswax tapers by tightly covering them with plastic wrap and storing them in the freezer. On sultry summer evenings, your candles will be less likely to sag and droop if they have been treated this way. Leave them in the freezer until your guests arrive or you are ready to light them.

2
Wash and dry a variety of colorful bell peppers. You can substitute any sturdy vegetable or fruit. Summer or winter squash, shiny red apples, crisp pears, or a head of cabbage can be used as a candleholder centerpiece.

3
Arrange the peppers on a platter or in a flat basket. If needed, use a bit of candle adhesive on the bottom of each pepper to anchor it to the platter.

4
Use the nail to make a small hole in a pepper. Don't push it all the way in. Fit a candle in the hole to check the size and alignment. Make the hole larger if needed.

5
Make holes in all of the peppers. Insert your chilled candles, and prepare to accept the appropriate accolades from your guests.

Light Shower Parasol

Designer
Terry Taylor

Tiny lights twinkle like glistening raindrops through this luminous paper parasol. If the dew point is high or the skies threaten to downpour, store your parasol in a covered spot to enjoy its romantic light on another evening.

What You Need

Paper parasol

100-bulb minilight strand

Floral tape

Floral wire

Extension cord

Scissors

Glue gun and glue sticks

Low-tack masking tape

What You Do

1

Open the parasol. If you are superstitious, you might want to work on this project outside! Position the plug end of the minilight strand at the end of the handle. Use the floral tape to secure the cord along the handle in several places.

2

Unwind a length of floral wire and cut it into several 4-inch (10 cm) lengths. Set the lengths of wire aside.

3

Place the parasol upside down on the floor or on a table. This makes it easy to rotate the umbrella as you position the light strand.

4

Wind the light strand around the stretcher of the parasol, fastening it with short lengths of wire. Give each wire a few twists to secure the strand.

5

When you have finished wiring the strand to the stretcher, spiral the rest of the strand out toward the edge of the parasol.

6

Use hot glue to attach the minilight strand to the ribs. Small strips of low-tack masking tape help position the strand on the parasol. Use the tape to hold the strand in place on either side of the rib where you plan to glue it. Leave the strips of tape in place until the glue has thoroughly cooled. Remove the strips.

7

Place the completed parasol in the garden, tucked behind low-growing plants or by the front entrance of your home.

Illuminated Strawberry Pots

Designer
Chris Rankin

On a warm summer evening, these strawberry pots blossom with light. Built-in pockets provide perfect ledges for tea lights— a charming accent for your patio or garden.

What You Need

Terra-cotta strawberry pots

Gravel or river pebbles

Tea lights

Smooth stones (optional)

What You Do

1

Purchase terra-cotta strawberry pots at a home or garden center. These pots come in various heights and widths—you can mix and match sizes for a tiered effect.

2

Decide where you want your pots to be before filling them—they'll be too heavy to move later. Fill the pots with river pebbles, gravel, or tightly packed soil. Sand doesn't work as a filler.

3

Tuck a tea light into each pocket of the jar, placing it as close to the edge of the pocket as possible. Placing the lights too close to the terra-cotta surface may result in soot stains. You can leave them in the metal cups or remove them for a more natural look.

4

In the top of the pot, arrange as many lights as you want, in or out of the metal cups. You may want to use different colored tea lights, or scatter smooth stones in the gravel for a decorative effect.

Bella Cucina
Tin Can Shades

Designer
Terry Taylor

Y ou don't have to go all the way to Italy to enjoy a romantic dinner *al fresco*. Hang a strand of these shades over your outdoor table, and let them transport you to *la bel'Italia*. Serve chilled pasta salad with tomatoes and olive oil, or match your shades to your meal. *Buon appetito!*

Tin cans*

Can opener

Light strand with candelabra bulb sockets

Large nail

Hammer

Marking pen

Tin snips

Half-round file

Handsaw

Small, motorized cutting tool

3 or 4 lengths of bamboo or bamboo garden stakes, each about 6 feet (1.8 m) long

Floral tape (optional)

Minilight strands (optional)

Cans with printed graphics rather than printed labels work best.

What You Do

1

Use the can opener to remove the bottom of each can. Store the contents of the cans or use them immediately to make supper. Wash and dry the cans thoroughly.

2

Remove the lightbulbs from their sockets. Center a light socket on the top of a can. Trace around the socket with the marking pen. Repeat for each can.

3

Punch small holes in the center of the marked circles using a large nail and the hammer.

4

Use the tip of the snips to enlarge the punched holes, then cut inside of the marked line. Don't cut too closely to the marked line—you don't want to cut the hole too large or the shade won't fit. File any sharp edges with the half-round file.

5

Place a shade on the socket, then reach inside the shade holding the bulb, and screw the bulb into the socket. Repeat for each socket on the strand.

6

Saw one end of each of the bamboo stakes at a sharp angle to make it easier to drive into the ground. Use the small motorized cutting tool to make ⅜-inch-deep (9.5 mm) notches on the flat end of the stake.

7

Drive the stakes into the ground and drape the light cord in the notches along the top of the stakes.

8

You may wish to wind additional light strands to the strand with the tin shades. For a finished appearance, wind floral tape around the light strands to join them.

Uplifting Lanterns

Designer
Robin Clark

A happy union of good looks and clever design, these handsome lanterns feature a smart solution for keeping candles lit on even the breeziest night. Simply lift the dowel at the top of the lantern to raise the candle for lighting, then lower it to keep the flame protected.

For one lantern

1 plank of western red cedar, 1 x 8 inches x 3 feet
(2.5 cm x 20.3 cm x 10 m); redwood, cypress, teak or Honduran
mahogany are suitable alternatives
1 fir or pine dowel, ⅜-inch diameter x 1 foot (9 mm x 30.5 cm)
4 pieces of "smoked" or tinted acrylic plastic, ⅛ x 5-½ x 8 inches
(3 mm x 13.8 cm x 20 cm)
4 deck screws, #6 x 1-¼-inch (3.2 cm)
8 deck screws, #8 x 2-inch (5.1 cm)
Medium-grit sandpaper
Clear exterior finish
Philips screwdriver
Small compass
Power drill with ⅛-inch (3 mm) and ⅜-inch (9.5 mm) drill bits; 2-inch (5.1
cm) spade bit; 3-inch (7.6 cm) hole saw bit
Circular saw with rip guide or table saw
Jigsaw or band saw
Router with ¼-inch (6 mm) round-over bit with pilot bearing
C clamps
Pillar candle, 2 x 6 inches (5 cm x 15 cm)

Cutting List

Description	Qty.	Dimensions
Top and bottom	2	¾ x 7-¼ x 7-¼"
Candleholder	1	¾ x 5 x 5"
Base	1	¾ x 5 x 5"
Posts	4	¾ x ¾ x 8"
Dowel	1	⅜ x 11"

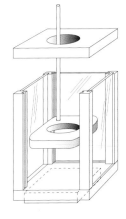

Figure 1

1

Cut the lantern parts, including the dowel, to the dimensions shown in the cutting list, using the circular saw or the table saw. If you can't find the acrylic sheets in the dimensions listed, have a hardware store or home center cut them to size.

2

Drill a 1/8-inch (3 mm) pilot hole 3/4 inches (1.9 cm) in from each corner of the top and bottom, and in the base. In the top piece, drill a 3-inch (7.5 cm) diameter hole through the center of the board. Use a scrap block of wood below to prevent tear-out as you drill. Drill a 2-inch (5 cm) diameter hole about 3/8 inch (9 mm) deep in the center of the candleholder blank.

3

Once you've drilled all the holes, center the base on the bottom and secure it with four 1-1/4-inch (3.2 cm) screws, driving them through the pilot holes in the base and into the bottom.

4

Center the candleholder blank on the top and clamp the two pieces together. Mark 1 inch (2.5 cm) in from one corner of the holder blank for the dowel hole. Then drill a 3/8-inch (9 mm) hole through both pieces. Unclamp and set the top blank aside.

5

Use the compass—set to a 2-3/4-inch (7 cm) radius—to lay out the rounded corners on the candleholder blank, and saw the corners with the jigsaw or band saw. Then use the router and the 1/4-inch (6 mm) round-over bit to round over all the edges on the lantern pieces, leaving the edges sharp where two parts join.

6

Put a dab of glue in the 3/8-inch (9 mm) hole you drilled in the candleholder and insert the dowel into the hole, tapping the dowel until it's flush with the bottom of the holder (see figure 1).

7

Now groove the posts for the plastic panels. Raise the blade on the table saw 1/4 inch (6 mm) above the table, and lock the rip fence 3/8 inch (9.5 mm) from the blade. (You can achieve the same set-up using a circular saw and a rip guide if necessary.) Push the posts over the blade, cutting a 1/4-inch-deep (6 mm) groove in two adjacent sides of each post. Be sure to use a push stick to keep your fingers clear of the spinning blade.

8

Attach the posts to the bottom piece with 2-inch (5.1 cm) screws, driving the screws through the pilot holes in the bottom and into the ends of the posts. Be sure to orient each post so the grooves are offset towards the outside of the lantern.

9

Before you install the plastic panels, apply a coat of clear exterior sealer to all the wood parts. Choose a sealer with UV and mildew inhibitors to help retain the natural color of the wood and deter mold.

10

Once the finish has dried, slide the acrylic plastic sheets into the grooves in the posts from the top of the lantern.

11

Lower the doweled candleholder inside the lantern, and slip the top over the dowel. Then secure the top to the posts by driving the remaining 2-inch (5.1 cm) screws through the pilot holes in the top and into the ends of the posts.

Tinkerbell Fairy Lights

Designer
Terry Taylor

A twist on the classic look of Victorian fairy lights, this modern and eco-friendly design will infuse your gathering with an ethereal glow. As night falls, string up green, amber, or cobalt blue bottles and transform your garden or porch into a magical realm.

What You Need

An assortment of glass bottles

Bottle cutter

Work gloves

Safety glasses

22-gauge galvanized wire, about 4 yards (5.5 m) long for each light

Wire cutter

Masking tape

Needle-nose pliers

General purpose pliers

Ruler

Broomstick or ¾-inch (1.9 cm) dowel, 12 inches (31 cm) long

Votives, tea lights, or candle fuel cells

Wire tomato cage

1

Remove all labels from the bottles and clean them with warm, soapy water. Allow the bottles to dry.

2

Following the manufacturer's instructions, use the bottle cutter to cut each bottle. Be sure to leave enough of an opening to insert a votive candle, tea light, or fuel cell. Wear heavy work gloves and safety glasses.

3

For each bottle, cut two lengths of the 22-gauge wire, each 36 inches (.9 m) long.

4

Cross the two wires to form an X shape and twist the wires together at the center. Turn a cut bottle upside down. Place the crossed wires on the bottom, and secure with a short length of masking tape.

5

Turn the bottle right side up. Use your fingers to smooth and shape the wires up the sides of the bottle. Secure the wires about halfway up the sides with masking tape. The four wires become your hanger wires. Set the bottle aside and repeat steps 3 through 5 for additional bottles.

6

Wrap a length of wire 20 or more times around the broomstick to make a coil. Keep the wire coiled tightly. Wind far more than you think you will need to wrap around the top of each bottle.

7

Remove the coil from the broomstick. Splay out the loops one by one, holding them firmly between your fingers and thumb. Keep splaying out the loops until

the entire coil is flattened. The loops will look slightly oval, but you can round each oval with your fingers.

8

Wrap the length of flattened coil around the top of a cut bottle. Use wire cutters to cut the length needed to go around the bottle from the coil. Set the extra coil aside.

9

Wrap the coil around the mouth of the bottle. Use your fingers and pliers (if needed) to wind a length of one of the hanger wires to a point on the flattened coil. Secure the coil around the bottle with the remaining three wires.

10

Repeat steps 8 and 9 for each bottle.

11

Gather the four wires together. Use your fingers to twist them loosely about 4 inches (10 cm) above the rim of the bottle. Hold the twist with the pliers. Use needle-nose pliers to tightly twist a 1-inch (2.5 cm) segment of the four wires together. Cut the excess, untwisted wire with the wire cutters. Make a simple hook with needle-nose pliers at the end of the twisted wires.

12

Repeat step 11 for additional bottles.

13

Push the legs of the tomato cage firmly into the ground, and hang your completed fairy lights on the support wires. Place votives, tea lights, or candle fuel cells in the hanging bottles.

Glitterbug Candle Shades

Designer

Jean Tomaso Moore

Charming, glittering night visitors alight on these terra-cotta flower pots to illuminate your porch, deck, or pathway. Make a dozen or so to add sparkle to the evening, or create just one as an outdoor table centerpiece.

What You Need

For each candle shade

Terra-cotta flowerpot, 8 inches (20.3 cm) in diameter

White acrylic craft paint

Gold spray paint

Gold acrylic craft paint

Decoupage medium

Spray acrylic sealer

Several sheets of white tissue paper

Black rubber stamp ink

Rubber stamps

Stamp pads

Foam brush or sponge

Duct tape

Scissors

Sand

12-inch (30.5 cm) taper candle

Glass hurricane chimney, 5 inches (12.7 cm) wide at the top and 12 inches (30.5 cm) high

What You Do

1

Sponge or brush slightly diluted white acrylic paint onto the outside surfaces of the flowerpot. Spray the insides of the pot with the gold paint and let dry.

2

Cover the inside bottom hole of the flowerpot with a small piece of duct tape.

3

Stamp multiple images from the rubber stamps onto a sheet of tissue paper. Create approximately 20 images using the black ink and about 10 images using the gold acrylic paint. You may have to repeat this step, depending on the size of the tissue paper.

4

When the images are dry, use the scissors to cut away any excess tissue paper.

5

Brush the decoupage medium onto each sheet of tissue paper, and adhere the sheets to the flowerpot in a random pattern.

6

Once dry, spray on several coats of clear acrylic sealer to protect your design from the elements.

7

Fill the pot two-thirds full with sand, leaving the duct tape over the inside hole.

8

Insert a taper candle into the sand, pushing it through the sand for stability.

9

Top the candle with a glass chimney.

10

Repeat these steps to create other candle shades, if more than one is desired.

Brilliant Bugs

Nothing heralds the arrival of summer like the first sighting of fireflies. Their flashing lights infuse a summer night with mystery and anticipation. We instinctively want to capture their beauty and understand their magic.

Fireflies, also known as lightening bugs, are nocturnal members of the beetle family. They are "bioluminescent insects," which means, of course, that they glow. Their blinking lights vary in color from yellow-green to red-orange. It's most commonly believed that their flicker accomplishes two things—it warns predators of the firefly's unpleasant taste, and it insures that a male firefly will attract his proper mate. The intermittent flashing that we see between fireflies is probably signals between male and females hoping to reproduce. Flashes come from a firefly's abdomen, where oxygen reacts with chemicals to produce light. Males flash first and females respond, generally with a flash about two seconds later.

There are over two thousand species of firefly. Preferring warm, humid climates, their greatest populations are found in Asia, and Central and South America. In the United States, flashing fireflies are rarely found west of central Kansas.

Nearly all of a firefly's radiant energy appears as light, whereas a normal electric light bulb emits about 10 percent illumination and 90 percent heat. The brightness of a single firefly flicker is only 1/40 that of a candle flame.

To attract fireflies to your yard, reduce or eliminate chemicals in your garden. Cut down on any nonessential lighting—fireflies chose when to flash according to the intensity of the ambient light. On a clear night with full moon, you'll see fewer fireflies. Low, overhanging trees, tall grass or similar vegetation, will provide adult fireflies a place to rest and remain cool during the day.

Made in the Shade Umbrella Lights

Designer

Chris Rankin

With a little planning and creative camouflage, you can turn a plain market umbrella into a cozy lighted canopy. The truly creative part of the project is disguising the unsightly light strand that runs up the umbrella's pole. Set your imagination free and change the look as you will.

What You Need

Market umbrella

1 or 2 minilight strands

Floral tape

Floral wire

Material to cover length of center pole: crepe paper, nylon netting, stiff silk gauze, or any lightweight fabric

Wire-edged ribbon, thick drapery rope, raffia, a strand of silk flowers or silk ivy leaves, or material of your choice

Scissors

Glue gun and glue sticks

What You Do

1

Open the market umbrella. Position the plug end of the light strand cord on the center pole. Thread the plug through the hole where the pole comes through the table. Use the floral tape or lengths of floral wire to secure the cord to the pole in several places.

2

Unwind a length of floral wire and cut it into several 4-inch (10 cm) lengths. Set the lengths of wire aside.

3

Use the short strands of wire to attach the light strand along the ribs of the umbrella. Thread a strand of wire between the rib and the canvas cover. Pull the light strand snugly against the rib and twist the ends of the wire tightly together.

Work out toward the edge of the umbrella, and then back along the same rib. Trim the ends of the wire or wind them behind the rib.

4

Pull the strand to an adjacent rib and repeat step 3. If you run out of lights, add an additional strand. Anchor the joined plugs tightly to the rib.

5

When all ribs are lined with light strands, run the excess length of the last strand down the pole. Tape or wire the strand to the pole. Do not pull the light strand through the hole.

6

Estimate or measure the height of your pole from the table to the stretcher of the umbrella. Cut a length of material to this size. Attach the material to the pole using the hot glue and wrap it around the pole. Wind your binding material up the pole and attach it along the fabric with hot glue. Create a taut covering or a gathered appearance. For a formal dinner, use a length of crushed velvet bound with thick drapery cording. You can achieve a dressier look with nylon netting tied with ribbons. For a casual summer party, loosely wind the pole with bright crepe paper tied with lengths of raffia.

Pipe Dream Candleholder

Designer
Chris Rankin

T ake a quick trip to your local plumbing supply store or a well-stocked home improvement center to buy the materials you'll need for this high-tech (but low-assembly) candleholder. You'll find a bewildering and fascinating array of copper plumbing parts to inspire a truly unique creation.

What You Need

Stand-off fixture (these come in a variety of sizes)

Female and male adapters

45° street elbows

Couplers

Reducers

Scrub pad (optional)

Commercial verdigris patina (optional)

Paintbrush (optional)

Taper candles

1

Choose a stand-off fixture. The shape of the fixture and the number and diameter of holes will determine which plumbing parts you will use.

2

Select two or more female adapters to support the stand-off. Space them along the length as desired. You can create tall arms by using two street elbows on two or more adapters.

3

Fit a variety of couplers, adapters, and reducers in the holes as desired. Once the candleholder is placed where it will be used, you can use it as is. If you wish to create a patinated surface, follow the next step.

4

The candleholder will develop the rich patina of rust and verdigris if you leave it outdoors. If you love the look of verdigris but don't want to wait for it to happen naturally, paint the copper plumbing parts with several coats of a commercial patina solution or follow the instructions on page 39. To quicken the patination process, abrade the copper surfaces with a scrub pad. This will remove any lacquer that may have been applied to the surface.

On the other hand, if the sheen of polished copper is just the look you're after, disassemble the candleholder and store it out of the weather.

Bright Harvest Gourd Lantern

Designer
Dyan Mai Peterson

Simple geometric shapes and jewel-like colors adorn this easy-to-make gourd lantern. Make just one for a dramatic lighted centerpiece, or several to dress up a deck or porch.

What You Need

Hard-shell gourd (choose one with a flat bottom)

Leather dyes in assorted colors

1-inch (2.5 cm) sponge brush

Basin with water

Metal kitchen scrub pad

Cotton swabs

Clear spray lacquer or clear acrylic varnish

Pencil

Sharp kitchen knife with serrated blade

Keyhole or hobby saw

Metal spoon

Fine-grit sandpaper

Wood burning tool with straight tip

Black felt-tip marker with medium tip

Power drill with assorted drill bits, 1/8 to 1/2 inch (3mm to 1.3 cm)

Battery-operated light fixture (see note on page 38)

1

Soak the gourd in warm water for up to 15 minutes, then scrub off any mold and dirt with the metal kitchen scrub pad. Allow the gourd to dry.

2

On the bottom of the gourd, sketch a square shape large enough to fit over your light source. Use the kitchen knife to make a hole on the marked line large enough to accommodate the blade of the saw.

3

Use the saw to cut along the line you have drawn.

4

Remove the piece of gourd and pull out all the loose pulp and seeds. Scrape out the pulp that is stuck to the interior shell with a metal spoon. You may wish to save the seeds for next year's gourd crop.

5

Sand the cut edge of the opening with fine-grit sandpaper.

6

Draw simple geometric forms on the gourd as desired, then add slightly larger, similarly shaped forms around the sketched shapes.

7

Heat the wood burning tool according to the manufacturer's instructions. Using a light touch, trace the sketched forms with the heated tool. Go over the lines until you're satisfied with the darkness of the burned line.

8

Use the foam brush and cotton swabs to paint the small forms with leather dye. Allow them to dry. Re-apply dye until you're satisfied with the depth of color.

9

Outline the colored form with the black marker if desired.

10

Coat the gourd with clear lacquer or acrylic varnish and allow it to dry. Repeat with a second coat if desired.

11

Drill a hole or two in each of the colored forms, alternating the size of the drill bits. Choose a different size bit and drill additional holes in each shape. Set the gourd over your light source when you have drilled holes in all of the shapes. The light will help you decide if additional holes are needed.

Note: Don't illuminate this gourd lantern with candles. Use one of the many portable, battery-operated lighting fixtures available at hardware, camping, and discount stores. If you want to use a candle, you'll need to remove a portion of the gourd's top for ventilation; then use only a small votive candle or tea light inside the gourd. Never leave a burning candle unattended.

Verdigris

After centuries of exposure to the elements, the ancient Greek copper and bronze statues that we see in museums often have a weather-worn patina that only adds to their beauty. To achieve the same effect without the wait, it's possible to use a chemical process called *verdigris*. Literally "green of Greece," the procedure ages shiny new copper, brass, or bronze to a blue or green hue through a simple, rapid chemical process. Buy a commercial verdigris kit at a craft-supply store or make your own solution to use at home by following these instructions. Take precautions throughout this process—vinegar and ammonia are extremely caustic, so it's important to work in a well-ventilated area and wear protective gloves.

What You Need

Non-reactive container

Wood shavings, shredded soft paper, and/or cat litter

Glass jar for mixing chemicals

Ammonia

Salt

Vinegar

Rubber gloves

Old towel

What You Do

1

In the container, assemble any combination of wood shavings, shredded soft paper, or cat litter.

2

For a blue finish, pour ammonia into the jar, followed by a generous sprinkling of salt. To achieve a green finish, pour vinegar into the jar and mix with salt. Moisten (do not soak) the dry materials with the mixture you're using.

3

Place the copper, brass, or bronze pieces into the mixture and cover it loosely with the towel. The process will take a few days.

NOTE: Be sure to aerate your metal pieces by occasionally turning them; the verdigris finish is caused by oxidation, so exposure to oxygen is critical.

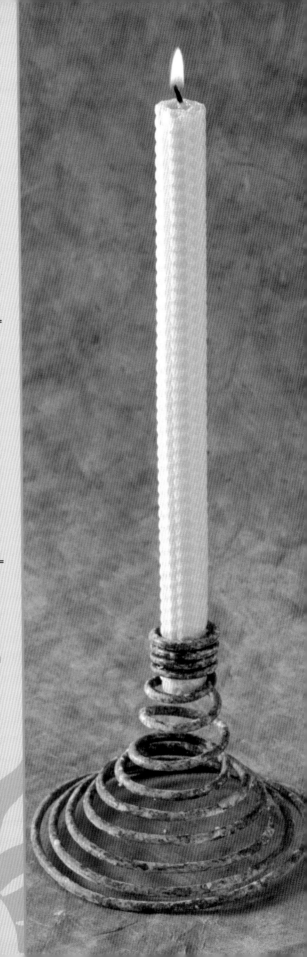

Great Balls of Fire Topiary

Designer

Terry Taylor

Like your flowers and foliage, this tasteful accent light can change

with the seasons. Choose light bulb colors that reflect the time of year:

orange for autumn, white for winter, green for spring, or red for summer.

Or, select colors to complement your garden blooms. Create a pair to

flank a walkway, or a bevy of twinkling balls for a festive event.

What You Need

Wire globe topiary form*

1 or 2 minilight strands

Floral tape

Extension cord

*The topiary form can be placed directly in the ground but may need to be shored up with a stone or brick to steady it. For a more permanent installation, anchor the form in a decorative terra-cotta pot filled with soil and planted with annuals.

What You Do

1

Wind the plug end of the minilight strand up the base of the form. Use floral tape in several places to secure the strand to the base.

2

Decide on the best arrangement for the minilights before starting to place them on the topiary form. You'll need to consider how tightly you want to string the lights and determine whether or not you need more than one strand. Attach the minilight strand to the wire ball with floral tape. Try to place the lights evenly around the ball. This can be accomplished by changing the direction in which you wind the minilight strand. Use floral tape to reinforce the attachment in the places you change directions.

3

To illuminate, plug the strand into an extension cord designed for outdoor use. You can use the floral tape to camouflage the cord and keep it from tangling. If you want the lights to blink on and off, you can buy a special fuse.

Copper Coil Sconce

Designer
Allison Smith

Candlelight glows warmly through the delicate spirals of this stylish copper sconce. This sophisticated design couldn't be easier to make—you only need a few twists of wire to produce elegant results.

What You Need

10-gauge copper wire, about 1 yard (91.4 cm)

14-gauge copper wire, about 4 yards (3.65 m)

18-gauge copper wire, about 2 feet (60.9 cm)

Wire cutters

Wooden spoon

Small glass votive candleholder and candle

For the Wall Hook

1

With the wire cutters, cut a 24-inch (61 cm) length of 10-gauge wire and fold it in half, crimping it at the end. Shape the end into a hook, creating an arch at the base of the hook to better support the weight of the candleholder.

2

Cut three 6-inch (15.2 cm) lengths of 14-gauge wire. Coil each length tightly around the bottom of the hook at varying intervals to hold it securely in place.

3

Shape the "open eye" near the base of the hook by bending the wires out to the sides at 90° angles, then bending them back to the center to form an oval.

4

Cut two 12-inch (30.5 cm) lengths of 10-gauge wire and position them on either side of the folded 24-inch (61 cm) primary wire. Join them to the primary wire by wrapping the three wires together with a 6-inch (15.2 cm) length of 14-gauge wire.

5

Coil the ends of all three pieces into spirals.

For the Sconce

6

Cut four 36-inch (92.5 cm) lengths of 14-gauge copper wire, and bend a loop into the center of each one. This loop will hold the top of the votive candleholder in place. Each loop should be the same size—slightly larger than the diameter of the glass votive. Don't use the whole length of wire to create the loop—you should have excess wire on either side of it.

7

Stack the loops together. The excess wire should radiate out from the center loop at different intervals to create four equal sections.

8

Cut a 24-inch (61 cm) length of 18-gauge wire and coil it tightly around the stacked center loops to hold them in place. Don't coil over the excess wires—work around them to make sure they remain loose and easy to move.

9

Take one length of excess wire from each of the four loops and pull it upward. Gather the four wires together, joining them about 6 inches (15.2 cm) from the center loop. Cut a 1-inch (2.5 cm) length of 14-gauge wire and wrap it tightly around the joined wires, making sure the coil you create is tight enough to prevent the wires from shifting.

10

At the top, make an eye loop by bending the shortest wire at a 90° angle about 1 inch (2.5 cm) down from the top, then bending the wire back upon itself. This is the loop you'll attach to the hanging wall hook.

11

Coil the remaining wires into spirals by wrapping them around the end of a wooden spoon.

12

Repeat steps 9 through 12 with the remaining wire, pulling downward instead of upward. The only adjustment you need to make to the instructions is that the distance between the center loop and the gathered coils on the bottom should be slightly smaller than the distance between the center loop and the top.

13

Set the votive holder in the center loop.

Lighted Terra-Cotta Planter Fountain

Designer
Susan Kieffer

The two most essential elements in a garden—light and water—are artfully combined in this soothing terra-cotta garden fountain. The underwater light subtly illuminates the fountain, highlighting the beautiful texture of the water-loving plants.

Terra-cotta planter bowl, 20 inches (51 cm) in diameter

Terra-cotta pot, 14 inches (36 cm) tall with 10-inch (25 cm) base

1-gallon (3.8 L) plastic milk container

Epoxy glue

Silicone caulk

Water sealant

Plastic knife

Scissors

Container for water

Rock or other heavy weight

Spray paint (optional)

Plastic plumbing coupling, 3 inches (8 cm) tall

Submersible pump

Bell fountain head

Small underwater halogen light kit

4-inch (10 cm) potted bog plant, such as umbrella grass (cyperus)

Floater plants, such as water hyacinth (eichornia)

Houseplant cuttings, such as spider plant (chlorophytum)

A handful of clear marbles or faux jewels

To Create the Fountain

1

Cut a flat 4-inch (10.2 cm) circle out of the plastic milk carton. With the plastic knife, apply the epoxy to the inside of the planter bowl, sealing the edges and covering the drainage hole. Weight down the plastic circle with a rock or other heavy weight until it's dry, about one hour.

2

Caulk the edges of the circle. Turn over the planter and fill the drainage hole and edges of the hole with about 1/2 inch (1.5 cm) of silicone caulk. Let the caulk cure for 24 hours.

3

Coat the interior of the planter with water sealant. Let it dry overnight. Apply a second coat and allow it to dry thoroughly.

4

If desired, spray-paint the exterior of the planter bowl and pot. Turn both of them upside down to spray-paint them.

5

Because the completed fountain is quite heavy and cumbersome, it's best to assemble it where it will be located. Make sure there is an electrical box with two three-pronged outlets within reach of the pump and lighting cords. Invert the pot to be used as the base, and center the planter bowl on top.

6

Set the pump on its lowest pressure setting, and place it in the planter bowl. Press it down so the suction cups secure it to the bottom.

7

Partially fill the planter bowl with water. Make sure the intake filter of the pump is covered. Attach the bell fountain spray head to the pump, plug in the pump, and adjust the pressure setting of the pump and spray head as desired. Unplug the pump.

8

Set the plastic plumbing coupling on the bottom of the planter bowl. Set the potted umbrella plant on the coupling. Place clear marbles or jewels around the stalks of the plant. Add water to the bowl; don't fill it to the rim.

9

Float the water hyacinths scattered around the pump and bowl. If the black, fibrous roots are long, cut them back to about 5 inches (12.7 cm) in length.

10

Use plant cuttings from a houseplant, such as a spider plant, to fill in among the plants. They will root easily.

11

Plug in the small halogen light and place the bulb in the water. You can place the light behind the fountain or behind the marbles surrounding the umbrella plant. Adjust the depth and location of the bulb for different effects. Unplug the light.

12

Before plugging in the fountain and light for extended use, create a drip loop in the electrical cords. Make a small loop in each cord about 2 feet (60 cm) from the fountain, and pass the plugs through the loop. This ensures that any water that might drip down the cords will not drip into the electrical outlet.

13

As a precaution, always unplug your fountain before leaving the house.

14

Check the water level of the fountain and add water if needed. Cover the intake filters of the pump by at least 1 inch (2.5 cm) of water. An occasional cleaning, perhaps every three or four months, will maintain good pump performance and rid all surfaces of algae and bacteria. Disassemble the fountain and wash the bowl with warm soapy water. Rinse and dry it well. Clean the pump following the manufacturer's recommendations.

Chande-Lerious Bicycle Wheel

Designer
Cathy Smith

Imitating the lines of its elegant crystal counterpart, this playful bicycle wheel chandelier uses bike parts, basic hardware, and a simple strand of minilights to shed some light on an outdoor room.

What You Need

Wheel

Inner tube

Minilight strand with candelabra bulb sockets

5-foot (12.7 m) length of bicycle chain

10 to 12 bicycle reflector strips, each 1 inch (2.5 cm) wide

Plastic spoke beads

Small, medium, and large bicycle sprockets

Cleaning supplies

Paper towels

Masking tape

Medium-grit sandpaper

Nylon wire ties

Silicone sealant

Industrial adhesive

Anti-rust enamel spray paint

Slat from a mini-blind shade

5-foot (12.7 m) length of electrical wire

Electrical wire plug

8-foot (25.4 m) length of medium jack chain

12 open S hooks

Small nonlocking carabiner

4-foot (15.2 m) length of small jack chain

Wire cutters

Pencil or felt-tip marker

Tape measure

Drill with ⅜-inch (9.5 mm) and ⅛-inch (3 mm) bits

Scissors

Hammer

Electrical wire splicer

Chain rivet extractor

Pliers (general purpose and needle-nose)

What You Do

For the Wheel

1

Remove all bearings, gear, and brake assemblies from the wheel. Clean dirt, rust, and grease from rims and spokes. If you're going to paint the wheel, lightly sand the inner rim to prepare the surface.

2

Remove the minilight bulbs from their sockets to prevent breakage. With the wire cutters, cut the last light from the strand, leaving a 2-inch (5.1 cm) wire tail at one end of the strand. Wind the strand snugly around the channel of the wheel, spacing tightly or loosely according to the desired effect. Mark the position of each bulb socket and remove the strand from the rim.

3

On the top of the wheel rim, measure and mark four equidistant positions for the hanging jack chains which will support the wheel. On the bottom of the rim, mark six equidistant positions for the decorative bike chain loops which will dangle below the wheel. Try to evenly space the chains and loops, positioning them to complement the spacing of the minilights.

4

Drill holes for the hanging chains and loops, using ⅜-inch (9.5 mm) and ⅛-inch (3 mm) bits respectively. Drill two more holes anywhere on the inner rim of the wheel with a ⅜-inch (9.5 mm) bit—these will be the entry points for the electrical wire. When you're finished drilling, use sandpaper to smooth out any rough edges around the holes.

5

To insulate the wires from the metal rim, line the bottom of the wheel channel with the inner tube. With the scissors, cut holes in the tube corresponding with the holes you drilled for the electrical wire.

6

Reposition the light strand, and wind it into the wheel channel, making sure that the lights are in the positions you originally marked. Secure the strand with wire ties. Cut the plug from the end of the strand with wire cutters. You should now have a 2-inch (5 cm) tail at either end of the strand.

7

Using the electrical wire splicer, splice the 5-foot (12.7 m) length of electrical wire onto the end of the strand that used to have the plug. Pull the end of the electrical wire through one of the holes you created in the inner tube and the corresponding hole in the wheel. Splice a short section of wire from the long wire and pull it through the remaining inner tube and inner rim holes. This short section will attach to the center cluster of lights which you'll create later. Tuck the free end of the light strand into the rim channel and seal it with silicone.

8

Cut the mini-blind slat into small pieces that will fit into the wheel rim between each light bulb socket. You should cut a sample first to make sure the width is correct and that the material snaps easily into the wheel rim with a little bending or sliding.

9

Cover the spokes and electrical wire with masking tape in preparation for spray-painting the wheel. Stuff the light sockets with paper towel to prevent paint from clogging the sockets. Paint the surface of the wheel, using two coats to cover all surfaces that are not protected by tape.

10

Glue the reflector strips to the outside of the rim at desired intervals using industrial adhesive.

For the Hanging Chains and Loops

11

Cut four 2-foot (61 cm) lengths of medium jack chain. Attach an open S hook to one end of each chain, then loop the hook into the holes you have drilled in the top of the wheel rim, repeating for each chain. Pull the four free ends of the chain together upward and thread them through the carabiner (see figure 1). Screw the clip closed to keep the chains in place.

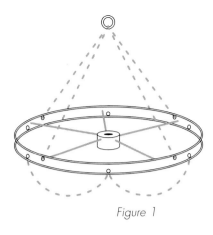

Figure 1

12

Fit six medium S hooks into the holes you drilled in the bottom rim. To create the hanging decorative loops, measure six identical lengths of bicycle chain (about 8 inches [20.3 cm] each), and use the chain rivet extractor to remove a link at the end of each length, leaving an open link on each end. Thread a small S hook through each open link, and attach to each medium S hook hanging from the holes in bottom of the rim (see figure 1). The chains will now hang as loops.

For the Hanging Chain Centerpiece

13

To create the hanging chain centerpiece, use the needle-nose pliers to cut the small jack chain into five 6-inch (15.2 cm) lengths (to suspend the large sprocket) and five 2-inch (5.1 cm) lengths (to suspend the small sprocket).

14

Decide which five spokes of the wheel you'll use to hang the chains from. Using the industrial adhesive, glue a plastic spoke bead to each of the five spokes about 2 inches (5.1 cm) from the rim. The spoke bead will prevent the chain from sliding up and down the spoke. Once the spoke beads are securely in place, attach a medium S hook to each spoke on the side of the bead closest to the rim. Hang a 6-inch (15.2 cm) length of small jack chain from each of the five medium S hooks hanging from the spokes.

15

To fasten the chains to the large sprocket, thread small S hooks through the center cutouts of the sprocket, and thread the hanging small jack chain through the top open end of the S hook. Tighten and close the top end of the hook with general purpose pliers.

16

Attach each of the five 2-inch (5.1 cm) lengths of small jack chain that you cut to the open bottom end of the S hooks. Tighten and close the bottom loop of the S hook. Attach the small sprocket to the end of the chains by threading the bottom link of each chain through a cutout in its center.

17

Wind the leftover bike chain around the rim of the large sprocket for decoration, using a hammer to pound one of the rivets you removed back into the open end links to join them.

For the Center Light Cluster

18

To create the center light cluster, cut a leftover section of the minilight strand containing three lights, and leave a 2-inch (5.1 cm) wire tail on each end. Cover one of the tails with silicone sealant. Splice the other end of the strand to the short spliced wire which is protruding from the wheel channel. Remove the bulbs from their sockets and push the assemblage down through the hub of the wheel. Replace the bulbs and cluster the lights together. Conceal the wires in the hub, and secure in place with nylon wire tie.

19

Weave the dangling electrical wire through the center of the wheel and tape it to one of the spokes with electrical tape to secure its place. Attach the plug.

Decked Out Candleholders

Designer
Rob Pulleyn

They usually play a supporting role on a deck or porch, but these decking posts really shine when they're cast in the lead as candleholders. Use one alone or create an ensemble to accompany your evening outdoors.

What You Need

Assorted deck posts and ornamental decking details*

Medium-grit sandpaper

Paint bucket

Paint mixing stick

Paintbrush

Water-based wood stain in blue or light green

Saw

Water

Hammer

Nails, at least 1½ inches (3.8 cm) long

Several large pillar and large votive candles

available at building-supply stores

What You Do

1

Cut the deck posts into varying lengths. You may need to saw off some rounded sides so that you wind up with a flat side on either end. Sand any rough edges.

2

Mix the colored wood stain with water so that you wind up with a very diluted tint. Apply three coats of stain, letting each coat dry. Used on treated lumber, which often has a blue or green color, the stain creates an appealing, weather-worn patina.

3

Hammer a single nail into the center of the top of each decking candleholder. The head of the nail should stick out approximately 1 inch (2.5 cm).

4

Keep the candle level and push it down securely onto the nail.

Uncommon Flare

Designer
Jean Tomaso Moore

Y ou may not recognize these plain tiki torches masked with broom bristles, leather cords, and beads. In this exotic disguise, they evoke sultry nights in the tropics.

Commercial bamboo torch with fuel canister and wick, 4 to 5 feet (1.2 to 1.5 m) high

2 twig brooms, each 36 inches (90 cm) long

3 lengths of sea grass, each 12 inches (30.5 cm) long

Raffia, about 3 yards (2.74 m)

22-gauge rust or dark-colored wire, 10 yards (9 m)

2-foot (60 cm) length of threaded metal rod

2-ounce (56 g) bottle of brown acrylic craft paint

Paintbrush

Multipurpose cutting tool, such as a hacksaw

Wire cutters

Glue gun and glue sticks

Ceramic, glass, or other natural beads

Feathers (optional)

What You Do

1
Paint the bamboo torch pole with the brown acrylic paint so it blends with the broom bristles. Let dry and set aside.

2
Cut the bottom (sweeper) off the broom with the cutting tool, leaving only the handle. You'll use the detached sweeper to cover the top of the torch, encircling the entire canister area.

3
Cut a 3-foot (7.6 m) length of wire. At the point where the canister and pole meet, attach the sweeper to the torch with the wire, wrapping it tightly to prevent it from falling off. Trim the excess broom bristles away from the canister to prevent contact with flames.

4
Cut the bristles off the broom handle and use them to conceal the torch pole. Attach the bristles to the pole with several 3-foot (7.6 m) lengths of wire wrapped tightly around the torch in a few different places on the pole.

5
Using hot glue, attach the sea grass to the torch pole at desired intervals.

6
Above the top of the sea grass, wrap and knot several strands of raffia around the pole. Pull some raffia strands from the knot and let them cascade down one side.

7
Split the raffia into several smaller strands. Decide on a design and thread the beads onto the strands, knotting the ends to secure the beads in place. If desired, place hot glue on the quill of a feather and insert the quill into the hole of a bead.

8
Hammer the threaded metal rod halfway into the ground, and slip the decorated torch onto the rod to hold it upright. If you prefer to insert the torch directly into the ground, leave the bottom 12 inches (30.5 cm) of bamboo pole free of broom bristles.

9
Fill the canister with oil following the manufacturer's instructions, and light the torch.

The Marvelous Minilight: Use It in Safety

Years ago, leaving your Christmas lights up past January would draw disapproving glances from your neighbors. Those tiny, twinkling lights were so strongly associated with the holiday season that using them well into the new year was taboo. These days, electric minilights have come off the Christmas tree and into the front yard, porch, deck, and every room of the house—no time of the year is off-limits for this versatile lighting accessory.

Minilights come in various sizes, shapes, and colors, from the tried-and-true strand of white lights to the exotic and outrageous: lights shaped like bell peppers, flamingos, or palm trees. They are the perfect accent light—easy to install and change, energy-efficient, and economical. All these attributes add up to a flexible lighting solution that lets you express yourself.

It's important to make safety a part of your planning anytime electricity is involved. Here are some suggestions to achieve minilight displays that are as safe as they are beautiful.

First, inspect your old light sets. Look closely for cord fraying and broken or cracked sockets. If in doubt, throw them out! Purchase only UL (Underwriters' Laboratories) approved light sets rated for outdoor use, and read the instructions carefully; they can be found on the box and on the cord. The directions will state how many light strands you can safely connect. This will keep you from overloading electrical outlets and extension cords—a major fire hazard. To safely power multiple light sets, a circuit strip is useful. Keep your outlets accessible for quick disconnection if necessary. Unplug a light strand before replacing a bulb. Don't overload wall outlets and extension cords, and never use indoor extension cords outside.

It's important that every light socket has a bulb intact before using a strand of minilights. Always unplug your strand before replacing any bulbs. Minilights produce much less heat than larger bulbs. Nevertheless, keep all light sets clear of combustible materials and disconnect the cord before leaving your home or going to sleep. Even though engineered for outdoor use, minilight sets cannot withstand prolonged exposure to winter weather. Keep outdoor strands out of puddles and banks of snow. Properly maintaining your lights will insure many years of safe enjoyment.

Glittering Glass-Topped Table

Designer

Terry Taylor

*L*ight the way to the dinner table with a sparkling strand of minilights. You and your guests will be flattered by the soft uplighting, and the tone will be set for an elegant soiree.

What You Need

Glass-topped table*

2 minilight strands, 50-bulbs each
(or one 100-bulb strand)

1 roll of removable duct tape

Extension cord

Any size and shape glass-topped table can be used.

What You Do

1

Unwind a 6-foot (1.8 m) length of the minilight strand. Place the plug end at the foot of one table leg. Position this table leg in the general direction of your power source—you may need to use an extension cord to reach it. Working under the table to attach the strand is easier when an extra pair of hands helps handle the strand. If you're working alone, set the rest of the light strand on the tabletop. Use 2-inch (5 cm) lengths of duct tape to secure the strand to the table leg.

2

Work with 6-foot (1.8 m) lengths of the light strand when outlining the circumference of the table. Attach the strand to the table with 1-inch (2.5 cm) lengths of tape. You'll need to be especially neat if your glass top doesn't have a wide metal edge. Tear off strips of tape equal to the space between bulbs. Firmly press these longer strips over the strand between the bulbs by running your fingers close to the strand. Unwind another length of the light strand and repeat until you have attached the entire strand.

3

Spread a lightweight tablecloth over the table or drape lengths of inexpensive, lightweight muslin or theatrical scrim yardage around the table's perimeter to diffuse the light that shines from beneath the table. Adorn the table with an eclectic array of candles and glassware.

Rubber-Stamped Luminarias

Designer
Nicole Tuggle

A simple, classic way to line a path or walkway, these luminarias can be adapted to suit any season by choosing a stamp image that reflects the time of year. Choose a leaf print for autumn or a floral motif for a summer garden party.

What You Need

White paper bags

Rubber stamp

Ink pads

Clean sand

Tea lights or votive candles in glass containers

image in more than one color, stamp one color on all of the bags. Then clean the stamp before printing a second (or third) color.

3

Print the stamp on the reverse side of each bag as desired.

4

Fill each bag with approximately 1 cup (200 g) of clean sand.

5

Place a lit tea light or votive candle in a clear glass holder in each bag. Make sure you extinguish the candles before leaving the house or going to bed. Do not allow the candles to burn unattended.

What You Do

1

Working on an uncluttered, flat surface will help give your stamped images a crisp edge. You can stamp each bag the same way or allow yourself some creative freedom.

2

Use firm pressure to stamp your image on one side of each bag. Re-ink the stamp as needed. If you choose to stamp the same

Champagne Gel Candles

Designer

Chris Rankin

Add a bit of bubbly fun to your dinner party with these festive gel candles. A few candles on a buffet or dining table add a playful touch to the evening's atmosphere. Just make sure your guests don't try to drink them!

What You Need

Champagne glasses

Candle gel*

Yellow gel dye*

Pan

White copy paper

Candlewick

Wood cooking skewer

Stove top

Baking soda (optional)

available in solid form in the candlemaking section of most craft-supply stores

What You Do

1

Heat the gel over low heat until it just begins to melt, stirring as little as possible. TIP: Don't overheat the gel. If a fire breaks out, don't use water to quench it.

Candle gel is mineral-oil based, so if it's heated beyond its flash point, you will need to pour baking soda into the pan, cover it with a lid, and remove the pan from the heat source immediately.

2

Add just enough yellow dye to lightly tint the gel to a pale champagne color. (Double-check the color by removing a small amount of gel on a spoon and placing it on a sheet of heavy white paper.) Add additional gel to the pan if the color is too dark, or additional dye if it's too light.

3

Pour the gel into the glasses and arrange the wick. Create extra bubbles by placing the wood skewer in the top ¼ inch (3 mm) of the gel and gently moving it around.

4

Trim the wick to ¼ inch before the first burning and after every subsequent burning.

Light Industrial Candle Shades

Designer
Terry Taylor

Give these hardworking industrial tie plates a chance to show their romantic side. Candlelight filters through their lustrous metallic finish, adding a sophisticated look to your outdoor dining table.

For one shade

4 tie plates*

7 mm lock washers, 1 to 2 dozen**

Empty jar lid

2 pairs of sturdy pliers

Masking tape

Votive or small pillar candle

*found in the lumber section of your local hardware store

**found in the fastener section of your local hardware store

What You Do

1

Remove all labels from the tie plates.

2

Align the holes of the tie plates. There is usually a slight variation in their positioning. Use a small piece of masking tape to mark the top of each plate. It will save you time when matching up the holes later on. Set the tie plates aside.

3

Using a pair of pliers, grasp a lock washer to one side of the split. Then, using the second pair of pliers, gently open the lock washer. Do this by bending it laterally rather than making it wider. For faster production, open one lock washer and try it out for fit before opening all the washers you will need for the shade.

4

Lay one tie plate on top of another, matching the taped ends. Slide the opened lock washer into a matching pair of holes in the tie plate. This generally calls for some fiddling about before you successfully join the two plates. You may need to widen the opening of the lock washer to make it easier to slide the washer through the holes.

5

Determine how many lock washers you'll need to fasten the four sides of your shade. You'll develop a rhythm as you open the washers needed to complete the shade.

6

Complete one side of the shade at a time, matching the taped ends as you go along. You are simply linking the tie plates to one another.

7

To finish the shade, close each lock washer, grasping each side of the split with a pair of pliers and gently returning them to a closed position. Set a votive (or other pillar-type candle) in a jar lid inside the shade.

Breeze-Proof Oil Lamps

Designer
Chris Rankin

Oil lamps light your outdoor evening with traditional charm and aren't affected by the breeze. If you don't have an oil lamp, create your own using a canning jar, an adapted oil lamp burner, and a glass chimney.

Oil lamp or recycled canning jar

Oil lamp burner

Paraffin-base oil

Citronella oil (optional)

Commercial oil lamp wick

Newspaper

1

Search flea markets, garage sales, and resale shops for blue-green canning jars. Be sure you purchase jars with threaded necks. Oil lamp burners, adapted to fit canning jars, can be found in hardware and lighting shops. Choose a glass chimney that complements the height of the jars you have chosen to use.

2

Select your lamp oil. You may want to burn a paraffin-base lamp oil rather than a kerosene-base oil because paraffin-base oils are less likely to create soot on the lamp's glass chimney. Fill the lamp with a citronella-scented oil if you are plagued by no-see-ums and mosquitoes.

3

Before filling the jars, cover your work surface with sheets of newspaper to absorb any spilled oil. Pour enough lamp oil to fill each jar halfway. Securely screw on the lamp oil burner. Allow time for the wick to become saturated with oil—about 20 minutes should be enough. Adjust the wick so that about ¼ inch (6 mm) protrudes from the burner. Light the wick and set the glass chimney on the burner.

4

Set these breakable lamps on a sturdy surface. Metal railroad-style camping lanterns can be hung on a sturdy, low-hanging tree limb or placed along the sidewalk. Traditional, pressed-glass oil lamps can be used outdoors with care.

Love Bugs Citronella Gel Candles

Designer
Chris Rankin

No outdoor gathering is complete without a few crawling creatures. The cute plastic ones in these playful candles substitute for the real ones, which are kept away by the scent of citronella oil. A fun accent for a casual gathering, these candles are guaranteed to get a few laughs.

What You Need

Small glass containers

Colorful plastic or ceramic bugs

Candle gel*

Tweezers

Citronella essential oil

Metal skewer

Saucepan

Candlewick

Bubble stick*

Stove top

Baking soda (optional)

*available at craft-supply stores

1

Melt a small amount of candle gel in a pan. Place the bugs in the gel and watch for bubbles. If no bubbles appear, use tweezers to remove the bugs one at a time, holding each one over the pan until the gel solidifies. If you do see bubbles around the bugs, leave them in the gel until they stop bubbling, stirring occasionally. Place bugs in the glass containers. TIP: Don't overheat the gel. If a fire breaks out, don't use water to quench it. Candle gel is mineral-oil based, so if it's heated beyond its flash point, you will need to pour baking soda into the pan, cover it with a lid and remove the pan from the heat source immediately.

2

Over low heat, melt enough gel to fill the containers; the gel must reach the highest temperature recommended by the manufacturer. Stir in three drops of essential oil for each candle you plan to make. Pour the liquid gel into the container over the bugs, then use the metal skewer to rearrange the bugs' placement if desired.

3

Arrange the wicks in the containers. Gently swirl the gel with the bubble stick to remove as many bubbles as possible, then place the containers in the refrigerator for several hours until the gel solidifies.

Fire and Ice Lanterns

Designer
Chris Rankin

W ho says you can only use ice lanterns in the dead of winter? These stunning lights are perfect for crisp nights in early autumn, or to beckon your guests to a dreamy midsummer night's dinner party.

What You Need

Large and small plastic containers

Plastic drink bottles in various sizes

Scissors

Gravel or stones

Greenery (fern fronds, ivy vines, large autumn leaves, evergreens)

Tea lights or small votive candles

What You Do

1

Begin by selecting which size and shape container you wish your finished lantern to be. The size of your ice lanterns is limited only to the size and availability of room in your freezer. Once you have made room in your freezer, gather up a few of the

many plastic containers that proliferate in your cabinets and use them to create ice lanterns in several shapes and sizes. The illustrated examples range in size from take-out containers to a plastic serving bowl and wastebasket. Choose a second, smaller container (a drink bottle works well for this) to fit inside the larger container.

2

Use scissors to cut off the top of the smaller container. Make this container about the same height as the larger container. Set it aside.

3

Fill the large container with water to a depth of approximately 1 inch (2.5 cm). Place the container in the freezer until solid.

4

Set the smaller container on the frozen water. Place gravel or small stones in the smaller container to anchor it to the bottom. Arrange greenery around the container. Fill the container with water and place it in the freezer. You may find it helpful to float ice cubes on top of the water to hold the greenery under water, but it's not necessary to do so.

5

Unmold your ice lantern with cool or lukewarm water. Remove the stones from the inner container, fill it with lukewarm water, and allow it to sit for a couple of minutes. The small container should slide right out with a gentle tug. Turn the large container upside down in the sink and run lukewarm water over it. Your lantern should slide out. Store the lanterns in the freezer until needed.

6

When the occasion calls for it, remove the lantern from the freezer and set a small tea light or votive candle inside.

Silvery Moon Light Shade

Designer
Jean Tomaso Moore

An ordinary electric porch light will bathe your porch in "moonlight" when you cover it with this heavenly aluminum shade. With this easy makeover, a light that usually serves security duty can step out in style. The shade filters the light, creating a lovely glow.

What You Need

Rolled aluminum flashing

Framing square or ruler

Grease pencil

Tin snips or metal shears

Safety glasses*

Protective gloves*

Templates on page 74

Scissors

Block of scrap wood

Large nail

Hammer

Rag

Disposable plastic cups

Gold and silver acrylic craft paints

Small paintbrush

18-gauge galvanized wire, 5 pieces, each 12 inches (30.5 cm) long

24-gauge copper wire, 5 pieces, each 6 inches (15.2 cm) long

Bent-nose pliers

Spray acrylic sealer

Assortment of large glass beads

Wear protective glasses and gloves while cutting and piercing metal.

Note: This light shade is designed to fit a traditional coach-style, wall-mounted porch light that measures 4 inches (10 cm) wide and deep. Measure your porch light and adjust the measurements as needed.

What You Do

1

Using the framing square and grease pencil, draw a 14 x 18 inch (36 x 46 cm) rectangle on the aluminum flashing. Cut out the rectangle using the tin snips.

2

Draw a horizonal line 8-1/2 inches (22 cm) across the long side on the bottom of your rectangle.

3

Use a photocopier to enlarge the templates on page 74 to fit the rectangle. Cut out the large crescent moon and place it in the center of the rectangle below the marked line. Trace around the design with the grease pencil.

4

Cut out the stars and planet templates. Arrange them around the large moon. Trace around these designs with the grease pencil.

5

Center the smaller moon template above the grease pencil line. Make sure the moon touches the line. Trace around the moon. Place a large star to the side of the moon, also touching the line. Trace the star with a grease pencil. Repeat on the opposite side. Make sure all three images sit directly on the horizonal grease pencil line.

6

Set the aluminum rectangle flat on the block of wood. Use the large nail and hammer to pierce along the outline of all the designs. Space your pierced holes evenly and pierce completely through the metal. Work slowly and carefully.

7

Use the tin snips to cut along the horizontal grease pencil line. When you come to the star and moon shapes, cut away the excess metal. Be sure to leave at least one point of each shape touching the line.

8

Use a rag to rub away any residual grease pencil lines. Pour a small amount of silver paint into a plastic cup. Paint the interior of both moon designs silver. Allow the paint to dry.

9

Pour a small amount of gold paint into a plastic cup. Paint the stars and planet shapes with gold. Allow the paint to dry.

10

Using your lamp as a guide, center the design on the lamp. Use a grease pencil to mark the center portion. Use the framing square or a ruler as a guide to make a fold for each side.

11

At the top of the shade, fold a corner of the metal to help hold the shade in place. Your lamp may require a smaller or larger fold. Hold the shade up to the lamp and estimate the amount needed. Fold one side, check for fit, and adjust the fold as needed. Fold the opposite side to match.

12

Use a nail, hammer, and block of wood to pierce a hole into the bottom back corners of the folded shade. Pierce five holes at the bottom edge of the center section.

13

Thread one piece of 18-gauge wire through each hole. Adjust the sides to tighten and create the base

of the shade. Twist the ends of the wire at each end to secure.

14

Spray the shade with clear acrylic sealer to protect the design.

15

Use the bent-nose pliers to create a small loop at one end of each length of 6-inch (15.2 cm), 24-gauge copper wire; then thread several glass beads onto the wire. Create a second smaller loop to hold the beads in place. Thread the top of the loop through the pierced hole and allow the beads to dangle.

16

To place the shade on the lamp, slip it up over the bottom of the lamp, loosening the folded edges at the top. The shade should hold itself in place.

Serenity
Lantern

Designer
Sherri Warner Hunter

Create a peaceful

oasis in your garden

with this lovely lantern.

Simplicity is the key to its

appeal. Based on a

classic Japanese design,

its gentle lines

encourage quiet

contemplation.

Cooking pot lid, or other round flat form

Bread-dough (or other bowl) with lid

2 plastic planters, one 3-gallon (11.35 L) and one the same height but 4 inches (10.2 cm) smaller in diameter

2-liter plastic soda bottle

2-inch-thick (5.1 cm) sheet of polystyrene foam insulation

40-pound (18143 g) bag of premixed concrete

Water

Plastic tub (for mixing concrete)

Small rock

Utility tape

Plastic bags

Leather gloves

Nontoxic spray lubricant

Utility knife

Handsaw or band saw

Kitchen knife

Rasp

Wire brush

Candle

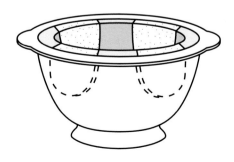

Figure 1

Note: Prepare all of your molds before mixing your concrete.

To Make the Molds

1

For the base of the lantern, decide what size you'd like the four support arches to be, and stencil the shapes onto the polystyrene insulation. Cut out these templates with the utility knife. With the flat edges of the arches facing up, line up the templates evenly with the rim of the bowl. Tape the polystyrene arch templates to the inside of the bread-dough bowl at equal intervals (see figure 1). After the arches are in position, spray the inside of the bowl with lubricant.

2

For the body of the lantern, cut four window arches from the polystyrene insulation and set aside until needed. Spray the inside of the larger plastic planter with the spray lubricant. Spray the inside and outside of the smaller planter with lubricant and set aside.

3

For the top of the lantern, spray the cooking pot lid or other form you selected with the spray lubricant and set aside until needed.

4

For the finial, cut the plastic soda bottle in half and discard the bottom half. Select a rock that will plug the opening of the bottle. Set aside until needed.

To Make the Lantern

5

Wearing the leather gloves, mix the concrete according to the instructions on the bag. Combine your premix material with enough water to keep it wet. Ideally, you want to have a crumbly texture that's just wet enough to hold together. Add concrete and water alternately until you get the consistency you want. You probably won't need to use the whole bag of concrete mix.

6

For the base, press the concrete firmly into the bowl, tapping to get rid of any air bubbles. The bottom of the bowl should be filled to about 3 inches (7.6 cm) thick. As you fill up the bowl, be sure to fill around the arch templates as you go. Build up the sides to about 2 inches (5.1 cm) thick and set aside.

7

For the body, press 2 inches (5.1 cm) of concrete into the bottom of the large planter. Center the smaller planter in the middle of the planter (with the open end facing up) and press down—there should be about 2 inches (5.1 cm) between the smaller and larger planters. Fill the space between the two planters with concrete until you get to the place where you want your window arches to be. Place the window arch templates, equally spaced, into the planter and secure them in place with tape (see figure 2). Continue to press in the concrete between the window forms, covering them as you fill the container to the top.

8

For the top of the lantern, firmly pack concrete into the lid or other flat form to create an even layer approximately 2 inches (5.1 cm) thick (see figure 3).

9

For the finial, pack about 3 to 4 inches (7.6 to 10.2 cm) of concrete into the bottle. Make sure the rock is in place, stopping up the mouth of the bottle (see figure 4).

10

Cover all the forms with plastic bags and leave undisturbed for a minimum of 24 hours.

11

Remove the pieces from the molds. In some cases, you may need to cut the mold to remove the piece.

12

Pull the plastic container out from the middle of the body casting and remove the polystyrene window shapes. Clean up the castings using the rasp, the utility knife, and the wire brush.

13

Hose the pieces with water, wrap them in plastic, and allow them to cure for five days.

14

Position the base on a level surface. Center the body with the opening upward, and place the candle inside. Center the top and then the finial.

Figure 2

Figure 4

Figure 3

Tea for Two Garden Torches

Designer
Terry Taylor

Don't let a fear of soldering stop you from making these whimsical garden torches. The tools and materials are easy to find. Before you begin, however, make sure your grandmother's heirloom sterling silver tea service looks better in the garden than on the sideboard! Use mismatched pieces if you can't find a matching set.

Silver-plate tea service (teapot, creamer, sugar bowl, tray)

Abrasive scouring pad

4 lengths of ½-inch (1.5 cm) copper pipe, each 5 feet (1.5 m) long

4 pipe couplers, ½ x 1 inch (1.5 x 2.5 cm)

Magnet

Hacksaw

Soldering and utility propane torch*

1 coil of lead-free solder

General purpose paste flux

Flux brush

2 firebricks

Pair of kitchen tongs

Bucket of water

Pillar or votive candles or candle fuel cells

*available in plumbing section of hardware store

What You Do

1

Purchase a silver-plate tea service at a flea market or tag sale. If you can't find a matching set, mix and match different patterns and pieces. Silver-plate nut dishes, cocktail shakers, or compotes will give you a different look. Make sure the service you purchase is silver plate—aluminum objects can't be soldered. Use a magnet to determine if your piece is silver plate or another material—it will be drawn to silver plate, but not aluminum.

2

Use the abrasive scouring pad to clean the bottom surface of each piece of silver plate, the edges and insides of the copper couplers, and the copper pipes. Clean surfaces are essential to successful soldering.

3

Place a piece of silver plate upside down on a firebrick. If there are handles on the silver plate, use both pieces of firebrick to support the silver plate and allow the handles to rest between them. Adjust the firebricks as needed to provide a sturdy support for the silver plate.

4

Brush a small amount of paste flux on the bottom of the silver-plate piece and the larger edge of a copper coupler. Set the coupler on the fluxed silver plate.

5

Unwind a 6-inch (15.2 cm) length of the coiled solder.

6

Follow the manufacturer's instructions concerning the use of the torch, and light it as directed. Hold the torch with one hand and the solder with your other hand. Aim the flame at the area where the coupler and silver plate meet. Allow the metal to heat for a bit. Put the end of the solder to the joint, and if the solder does not flow, continue heating the joint. The solder will flow when the joint is heated to the proper temperature. When the solder flows around the joint, remove the flame and turn off the torch. Allow the soldered joint to cool for several minutes. Use tongs to pick up the piece and place it in the container of water to ensure that it is cool enough to touch.

7

Repeat the procedure as needed for the number of silver-plate pieces you want to solder.

8

Use the hacksaw to make an angled cut at the bottom of each length of copper pipe.

9

Place a soldered piece of silver plate on the bricks as in step 6. Flux the small end of the coupler and the uncut end of a length of pipe. Place the pipe on the coupler and solder the two together. Allow the joint to cool before picking up the piece. Heat will be conducted up the length of the pipe, so the entire piece will be hot—be careful!

10

Repeat step 9 as needed to complete the desired number of torches.

11

Push the sharp end of the torches into the ground. Place pillar candles, votives, or fuel cells in the containers, and enjoy a twilight tea party.

Floral Watering Can Lantern

Designer
Anne McCloskey

The vibrant colors of this lantern guarantee that it will become a perennial favorite. In a few simple steps, this ordinary watering can is transformed into a garden lighting sensation.

Large metal watering can

Acrylic paints in yellow, yellow-orange, pink, purple, and lime green

Acrylic gloss varnish

Black felt-tip marker

Paintbrushes

Sponge brush

Medium-grit sandpaper

Paper towels

Wood block to fit inside watering can

Power drill with spiral-cut bit or ⅛-inch (3 mm) bit

Center punch

Pillar candle or votives

1

Start with a clean, dry watering can. Sand the entire can with sandpaper, wiping off the loose particles with a damp paper towel.

2

Apply two coats of yellow paint to the body and handle. Let dry.

3

Paint your flower design. The design shown here is a mixture of freehand circles, petals, and dabbed sponge-brush blotches. When the paint is completely dry, apply two coats of acrylic gloss varnish.

4

Decide where you want to drill holes in the watering can and use the black marker to mark them. The best places for holes are around the flowers. The more holes you make, the more candlelight will shine through the can.

5

Use the center punch to mark the points to be drilled.

6

Place the block of wood inside the can while drilling; this prevents the can from collapsing. Use the drill and bit of your choice to drill holes at the marked points.

7

Place small votives or larger pillar candles in the watering can, or use a citronella candle to keep bugs away on warm summer evenings.

Once-Upon-a-Lily-Pad Candle Shade

Designer
Diana Light

This dreamy painted glass shade evokes a fairy tale ambience when lit with a flickering candle (perhaps this frog really is a prince!). Using the patterns provided, it's simple to make and a pleasure to use on your deck or patio. When the weather turns cold, bring your shade indoors and enjoy it as a centerpiece on your dining table.

Clear glass hurricane shade

Commercial glass cleaner

Paper towels

Patterns on pages 84 and 85

Scissors

Cellophane tape

Cotton swabs

Isopropyl rubbing alcohol

2 cotton bath towels

Gold relief outliner*

Transparent glass paints (green, blue, orange, and yellow-green)*

Matte medium glass paint (gives the surface the look of etched glass)*

Gloss medium glass paint (lightens and thins paints)*

Small and medium-size paintbrushes

Small plastic containers

You may use either air-dry or oven-bake paints. Make sure all paints and mediums are the same type.

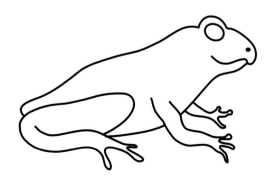

1

Remove any labels or stickers from the hurricane shade. Use the commercial brand glass cleaner to clean the glass. Allow to dry.

2

Enlarge the patterns on page 85 to fit your glass shade. Cut them out, leaving a ½-inch (1.3 cm) border around each pattern.

3

Position the patterns as desired on the interior of the shade, and tape them to the glass.

4

Fold each bath towel in half lengthwise and make two rolls. The two rolls will serve as padded supports as you paint the hurricane shade (it's easier to paint the shade when it's lying on its side).

5

Use the gold relief outliner to trace the outline of the patterns. Don't drag the tip of the outliner on the glass. Keep the tip a little above the glass and allow the line of paint to fall on the glass. If you make a mistake, use a cotton swab to clean it up. Allow the outlines to dry before you rotate the shade.

6

Dip a cotton swab in alcohol and clean the interior of the outlined shapes to get rid of oils and fingerprints before filling them in with color. Allow the glass to dry.

7

Mix a small amount of green paint with a little matte medium. Use a small to medium brush to fill in the lily pad shapes.

8

Brush undiluted matte medium onto the outer petals of the waterlily blossoms and the dragonfly wings. Leave the tiny interior sepals of the waterlily blossom unpainted.

9

Mix some orange paint with matte medium. Use a small brush to paint the interior sepals of the waterlily, the dragonfly body, and the eyes of the larger frog.

10

Blend yellow-green paint and matte medium. Paint the bodies of both frogs with this color.

11

Allow the paints to dry thoroughly. Before proceeding with the next step, clean the unpainted glass with alcohol-saturated paper towels and allow it to dry. This will remove any fingerprints and body oils that have stained the glass in the previous steps. It's important that the glass be absolutely clean to allow smooth application of the background paint.

12

Mix the blue paint with some gloss medium. Use a large brush to paint the spaces between the figures. You may find it easier to hold the piece by placing your arm through the shade, rather than having it rest on the towel rolls while you paint it.

13

Allow the paint to dry thoroughly. If necessary, bake the paint according to the manufacturer's instructions.

Flourless Cake Pan Sconces

Designer
Terry Taylor

When your cake pans are ready to retire from kitchen duty, give them new life on the patio or in the garden. They'll serve up a delicious glow of candlelight—the perfect accompaniment to your outdoor activities.

What You Need

For each Sconce

Round layer cake pan, 2-½ inches (6.4 cm) deep

Pattern template on page 126

Scissors

Rubber cement

Black felt-tip marker

Adjustable clamps

Small metal jar lid (baby food jar lids work well)

⅛-inch (3 mm) medium pop rivets

Pop rivet tool

Center punch

Drill with ⅛-inch (3 mm) bit

Scrap length of 2 x 4, about 6 inches (15.2 cm) long

L hook, 3 inches (8 cm) long

Tea light

1

Enlarge the pattern template on page 126 to match the diameter of your cake pans. Your sconces may have matching patterns or create a different one of your own.

2

Cut out the pattern templates and glue them to the bottom side of the cake pans with rubber cement.

3

Secure a cake pan, bottom side facing up, to your work surface with one or two adjustable clamps.

4

Use the center punch to mark each point on the pattern. This will prevent your drill bit from slipping when you drill the holes.

5

Secure the ⅛-inch (3 mm) bit in the drill. Use the drill to create the punched holes at each point in the pattern. Unclamp the pan after drilling all points of the pattern.

6

Decide where the top of the sconce will be when you hang it. Use the marker to make a mark near the rim. Secure the pan with clamps to the scrap of 2 x 4 and your work surface. Punch, then drill a hole at the marked point. Unclamp and rotate the pan. Mark, punch, and drill a second hole opposite the hanger hole you have just made, centering this hole on the side of the pan. Unclamp and set the pan aside.

7

Mark the center of the jar lid with a center punch. Drill a ⅛-inch (3 mm) hole. Use the pop rivet tool to rivet the lid to the second hole you made in step 6. The riveted lid is your candleholder.

8

Create ventilation holes for the candle on the side of the pan. Mark a single row of evenly spaced points around the side of the cake pan. Or, for a more decorative pattern, make short vertical rows of points or a wavy line around the side. After marking, punch the pattern and drill the holes.

9

Make a second sconce following steps 3 through 8, if desired.

10

Hang the sconces on an L hook on a wall, deck, or fence post.

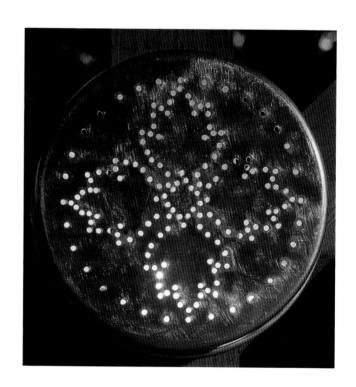

Chiminea— The Outdoor Fireplace

When night settles in but you're not quite ready to head indoors, the warm and fragrant chiminea, or patio fireplace, will let you savor outdoor living for hours longer. Its glowing embers set just the right mood for an evening under the stars.

The chiminea originated in seventeenth-century Mexico for cooking and heating at outdoor festivals. Crafted from terra-cotta clay, the chiminea is great for deck, patio, or pool parties and cookouts. Should conversations lag, pick a few sticks from around the garden, bring out a bag of marshmallows, and see what happens.

Chimineas burn wood, charcoal, or fire logs. Hardwoods such as oak, birch, and maple make less smoke than pine. Cedar and piñon woods are best for outdoor entertaining as they emit a sweet fragrance while burning. The smoke from piñon wood also acts as a natural mosquito deterrent.

Chimineas should be placed in a safe area away from flammable objects. Place 2 to 4 inches (5 to 10 cm) of sand or river rock in the bottom of a new chiminea for stability. This will also keep heat from drafting downward onto a wooden deck or patio. If the chiminea sits on a flammable surface, use a fire mat to protect surrounding areas from possible sparks.

Patio fireplaces require little care. The chiminea is easily cleaned using a regular fireplace shovel. Always leave some ash in the bottom to create a base for the next fire. A high heat fire may effect color changes in the terra-cotta. This is normal and necessary to bring out the fireplace's natural patina. Small hairline marks that appear due to firing are also routine. Occasionally rub your chiminea with an acrylic floor wax to maintain its original sheen.

Refined
Luminaria

Designer
Heather Smith

An upscale interpretation

of the classic paper bag

luminaria, this design

combines heavy-duty

hardware cloth with delicate

handmade paper to showcase

the gorgeous glow of a single

votive candle.

For one luminaria

Measuring tape

Scissors

Spray adhesive

¼-inch (6 mm) metal hardware cloth,* about 2 yards (1.82 m)

Assorted sheets of translucent handmade paper

Glass votive holder and candle

Most hardware stores will cut the length to your specifications.

What You Do

1

Decide how wide and tall you would like the finished luminaria to be. Allow for at least 2 inches (5 cm) of space around the votive, ensuring the flames won't contact the paper wall of the luminaria. Multiply the width of one side by four, add an extra ½ inch (1.3 cm) to overlap the ends, and measure this distance across the metal cloth. Mark your measurements on the metal cloth, and cut out the rectangular shape with scissors.

2

Subtract ½ inch (1.3 cm) from one end of the rectangle and divide the rest into equal quarters. Fold the rectangle at each quarter mark to form an upright cube. Bend the extra ½ inch (1.3 cm) of metal over the adjacent edge to close the cube. The top and bottom of the cube should be open.

3

Hold the handmade paper up to a lamp or window to make sure it's thin enough to allow light to pass through it. Measure enough paper to cover the cube, including an extra ½ inch (1.3 cm) along the top, bottom, and one edge to overlap the frame. Cut out the paper.

4

Spray the metal frame with adhesive and fold the paper around each side, smoothing it with a firm hand as you go. You should have a seam where the paper overlaps; spray a bit more glue here and press firmly. Fold the extra paper over the top and bottom of the cube to create neat borders around the openings.

5

Place the luminaria over a votive holder. When in use, the candle should be set in a holder in the center of the luminaria with at least 2 inches (5 cm) of space between the votive holder and each of the paper walls.

Flower Vase Candle Shades

Designer
Chris Bryant

Rekindle the joy of receiving flowers with this simple yet rewarding project. Long after the flowers have faded, the vase they came in will continue to bring you cheer. An eclectic mix of vases and other glass vessels with patterns creates an imaginative lighting display.

Commercial glass cleaner

Old glass flower vases

Assorted candles

Brown or white vinegar

Uncooked rice or beans

Plastic lid

1

Geather your flower vases and clean them. The glow from candlelight looks best when seen through vases with embossed surfaces of pressed glass—the motifs will be magnified and cast dramatic shadows. Add jam jars, tumblers, condiment bowls, or salt cellars with interesting relief patterns if desired.

2

Group your vases to develop intriguing silhouettes. Turn up the candlelight and accentuate the patterns by using a mirror as the base for your display. Using colored glass accents, such as cranberry or cobalt vases, adds interest to your setting.

3

Match your candles to the height and width of the vase, light, and enjoy!

4

At the end of the evening, use the following method to clean any soot stains that may have formed on the inside of the glass: Pour brown or white vinegar into the vase to cover the stain. Allow it to stand 30 minutes. Before emptying out the vinegar, add about ½ teaspoon (2.5 g) of dry, uncooked rice or six to ten dry beans. Cover the opening of the vase with an improvised lid and shake the vase rapidly so the hard grains rub off the loosened stain. Pour out the substance and rinse with water. Repeat if necessary.

Stamped Vellum Minilight Shades

Designer
Nicole Tuggle

Translucent vellum makes the perfect minilight shade—it's weighty enough to hold a folded shape but sheer enough to let the soft light shine through. This design is sophisticated but easy to make. Use different colored sheets of vellum to add interest.

1 sheet of card stock or stiff paper, 8-½ x 10 inches (21.6 cm x 26.7 cm)

25 sheets of vellum, each 8-½ x 10 inches (21.6 cm x 26.7 cm)

Pencil

Template on page 125

Ruler

Scissors

Craft knife

Butter knife or bone folder

Rubber stamp

Black ink pad

White craft glue or glue stick

Medium-size paintbrush

Transparent tape

Strand of 50-bulb minilight strand

What You Do

1

Use the template on page 125 to create a template on your 8-½ x 10-inch (21.6 cm x 26.7 cm) sheet of card stock. Outline the shape, and copy the dotted lines onto the template using a pen or pencil. Use a ruler for accuracy, and use the template to create all the shades.

2

Place the template on a sheet of vellum. Transfer the outline of the template on your vellum by tracing it with a pencil. Cut along the edges of your template with scissors or a craft knife.

3

Using a butter knife or bone folder, score your vellum sheet along the dotted guidelines copied from the template.

4

Continue steps 1 through 3 for all remaining sheets of vellum until you have cut, scored, and unfolded 25 shades.

5

Ink your rubber stamp well, and press it on to all four side panels of the shade. Allow the ink to dry for approximately 30 minutes.

6

Once the ink has dried, begin folding each shade along the edges until you have a rectangular box shape. There will be a small flap at the side. Overlap this flap with the joining edge (the larger flap should be on top) and glue down (see figure1). Because vellum is transparent, be sure to use only a thin layer of glue so it won't show through (using a glue stick helps avoid this problem). Let the glue set for 30 minutes.

7

Thread the shades onto a strand of lights, placing one over every other light bulb. Gently tuck each bulb under the flaps, allowing it to hang centered in the shade. Tape the top edge shut with transparent tape. Repeat with remaining shades.

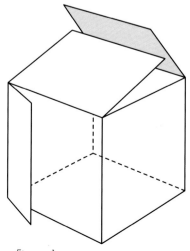

Figure 1

Re-envisioning Landscape Lo-lights

Even the most well-maintained gardens may have a few imperfections—a stubborn outcropping of rocks, a garden patch with more than its share of shade, a tree stump that trips up an otherwise level lawn. While you may want to camouflage these areas during the day, nightfall offers an opportunity to accentuate them with lighting. Art Director Dana Irwin transformed an unsightly tree stump (below) into an attractive candle platform with a few finishing nails and a variety of candles. A dark corner of her garden got a dramatic make-over with the addition of some simple metal pipe candleholders driven directly into the ground (lower right). The varying height of the pipes adds interest to the area, and their long, narrow silhouettes echo the shape of nearby trees. The unusual growth pattern in this tree (upper right) is stunningly lit with a single candle held in a coiled 22-gauge wire candleholder.

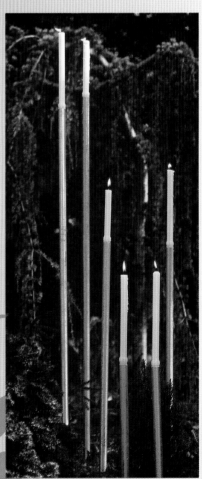

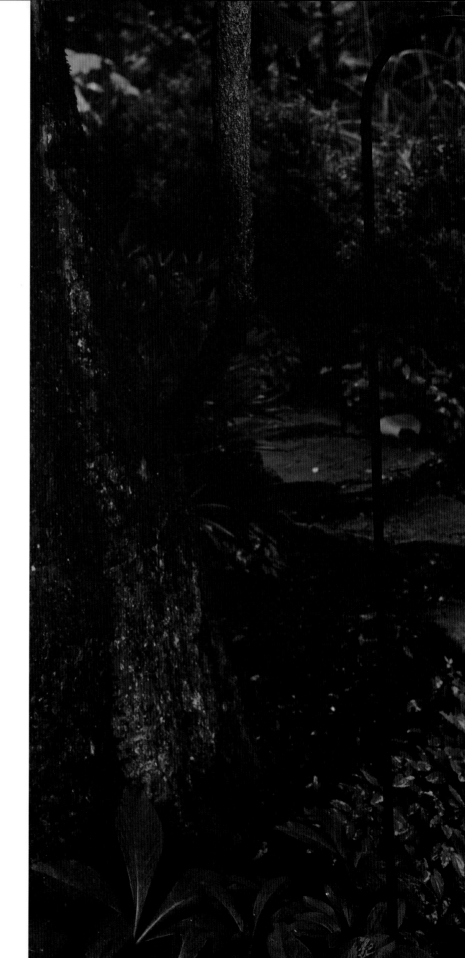

Natural Beauty Etched Glass Lantern

Designer
Diana Light

Delicate fern fronds provide ready-to-use stencils for etching a portable lantern. For a different look, try other types of plant material growing in your own backyard: maple or oak leaves, dried coarse grasses, or bamboo leaves all cast lovely shadows when candlelight illuminates their shapes.

Lantern with flat glass panels

Dried and pressed plant material

Paper towels

Glass cleaner

Several sheets of copy paper

Adhesive spray

Cotton swabs

Newsprint to cover work surface

Craft sticks

Glass etching cream

Heavy book (dictionaries are great)

Ruler

Pencil

Craft knife

Small squeegee with a blade, 2 to 3 inches
(5 to 7.5 cm) wide

What You Do

1

Take a walk in the woods or around your
neighborhood. Gather a variety of leaves, grasses,
and fern fronds. Don't limit your selection to just one
plant type: inspiration may strike when you see the
variety of dried plant material you have to work with!
Gather enough plant material for all of the panels of
your lantern.

2

Place a single layer of plant material on a paper towel. Cover the layer with another towel and press the plant material between the pages of a heavy book, such as a dictionary. Allow the leaves to dry for at least three days.

3

Measure one of the lantern's glass panels with the ruler. Use a pencil and ruler to draw a panel to size on the copy paper.

4

Carefully remove the plant materials from the book. Arrange the leaves on the copy paper. Play with placement and design ideas. Use the craft knife to trim the plant material to fit the panel if needed. If you want a frond or leaf to wrap from one panel to the next, use a craft knife to cut the piece. Once you've settled on a design, remove the leaves and sketch the placement for future reference. Don't throw away the dried materials you didn't use! You'll need them for the rest of the lantern panels.

5

Clean the lantern panels with the glass cleaner and allow them to dry thoroughly.

6

Place only enough dried plant material for one glass panel on the newsprint. Coat the flat side of the leaves with spray adhesive. Refer to your sketch to position the leaves on one glass panel. Press the leaves firmly to the glass, paying particular attention to the edge of the leaves.

7

Use a cotton swab moistened with water to wipe off any excess adhesive residue from the glass.

8

Cover your work surface with newsprint. Stir the etching cream thoroughly with a craft stick, then spread the cream evenly over the glass panel with a small squeegee.

9

Follow the manufacturer's instructions to determine the length of time you need to leave the cream on the glass.

10

When the time has elapsed, scrape the excess cream (if it's reusable) back into the container. Remove the dried plant material. Rinse the panel under running water and dry it.

11

Repeat steps 6 through 10 for each glass panel.

Retro-fit Chandelier

Designer
Susan Kieffer

This dazzling project offers a savvy re-use for that fizzled electrical fixture cast away after your dining room makeover.

Branched, electric light fixture

Wire cutters

Needle-nose and flat-nose pliers

Screwdriver

Metal snips

Candles

What You Do

1

Cut the plug from the end of the electrical cord. Use the pliers and wire cutters to remove the light sockets. Cut the electrical wire connected to each socket. If the wire will not easily move when you tug the cord, leave it in the fixture, but use wire cutters to cut the cord so it won't be seen.

2

Select the type of candle that will fit your fixture. Tapers may be appropriate for some chandeliers. In the project illustrated, the metal bobeche holds a short votive candle quite well.

Simple Pleasure Candle Pots

Designer
Sheila Ennis

These container candles are easy to make and add a refined beauty to your garden. Paint the pots in colors that accent your garden, and fill them with candles in complementary shades. A cluster of pots produces plenty of light to illuminate your evening on the porch or patio.

Terra-cotta pots and saucers

Several paintbrushes, one small with soft bristles

Burgundy acrylic spray paint

Silver or aluminum leaf*

Raw umber acrylic paint

Acrylic medium or glazing liquid*

Crackle glaze*

Light green (celadon) latex semi-gloss paint

Fine-grit sandpaper

*sold in art-supply stores and most craft-supply stores

What You Do

For the Silver Leaf Pots

1
Spray the entire pot (inside and out) and the saucer (if you're using one) with burgundy acrylic spray paint, and let dry thoroughly.

2
Apply the metallic leaf, following the directions on the package. The adhesive can be applied with any brush, but use a soft-bristle brush for the metallic leaf application. Use the leaf sparingly—don't put any on the lip or inside of the pot. TIP: Don't completely cover the area with metallic leaf; leave some blank spots so the undercoat color comes through.

3
Sand the pot very lightly—just enough to knock the shine off the leaf. You want to create the effect of old silver, not stainless steel.

4
To create a translucent glaze mixture, dilute a small amount of raw umber acrylic paint with the clear medium. Don't put much color in the glaze; you want a very light tint. Too much color gives the pot a dull look. Apply the raw umber glaze and let dry.

For the Crackle Pots

5
Apply the crackle medium to the outside of the pot and the saucer; let it set until the medium is tacky to the touch.

6
Apply the green semi-gloss latex paint. Try to be uniform in your brush strokes. The paint will crackle, revealing the terra-cotta finish underneath. Let dry.

7
Sand out any patchy areas. Sand all the edges to give the pot an aged look.

8
Apply the raw umber glaze, if you desire. Here again you want just a lightly tinted glaze. Let the glaze dry.

Making Container Candles

Container of your choice

Paraffin wax, approximately ½ pound (228 g)

Double-boiler setup

Knife

Candy thermometer

Candle dye (optional)

Scented oil (optional)

Mold sealer (optional)

Wick tab

Wire-core wick

Straightened length of wire coat hanger

Ladle or metal cup with a handle

Thin nail

Scissors

What You Do

1

Make sure the container will stand up to hot wax by filling it with near-boiling water; if it holds up to this temperature, it will work. Heat water over medium heat in the bottom of a double-boiler. Chop the wax into pieces with a knife and place the wax pieces in the top of the doubleboiler.

2

Heat the wax until it reaches 160° to 180°F (70° to 82°C). Don't let the wax get too hot. The flash point (the point at which wax will ignite) varies for different types of wax; make sure you know the flash point for your wax. If you're coloring the candle, melt the dye separately, then add it to the melted wax. Add any scented oils to the wax at this point, if desired.

3

If your container has a hole in it, fill it in with mold sealer. Cut a piece of wick to fit the container. When the wax is completely melted, dip it into the wax. When the wick has cooled, secure one end to a wick tab.

4

Turn off the heat. Wearing rubber gloves for insulation, warm the outside of the container by holding it under warm tap water for a few moments to prepare it for the temperature of the melted wax.

5

Pick up the container in one hand and pour a small amount of melted wax into the bottom of the container. Use the coat hanger to press the wick tab firmly into the wax. Pour in a little more wax to completely cover the wick tab. Position the coat hanger wire across the top of the container, and wrap the other end of the wick around it to keep the wick centered. Using a metal cup or ladle, pour the wax into the container until it's filled.

6

As the candle cools, a small well will form in the center of the candle. Check the candle until the well forms, then pierce the wax around the wick with a thin nail, being sure to pierce all the way to the bottom of the container. Bring the wax back up to pouring temperature and fill the well with melted wax. Repeat this process until a well no longer forms. Allow the candle to cool completely, then trim the wick to ½ or ¼ inch (1.3 or 6.cm).

Hoop Candleholder

Designer
Murray Spencer

A takes-your-breath-away hanging candle hoop is not for the faint of heart—it requires an outdoor space with large, impressive trees—not to mention a trio of willing and able friends to hoist it up or down.

Iron hoop or recycled barrel hoop

Electric drill and bit

Nail or screw

Calculator

Length of ⅛ to ³⁄₁₆-inch (3 to 5 mm) uncoated steel cable or vinyl-coated wire clothesline

Snap link

2 ferrules and stops sized for the cable you're using

Ladder (optional)

Note: If you don't have a sturdy oak limb that is 30 feet from the ground, adapt the directions and use a smaller hoop and vinyl-coated wire clothesline. The hoop pictured is about 5 feet (1.5 m) in diameter and hangs from a thin steel cable. Even a smaller hoop will take your breath away.

What You Do

1

To determine the length of steel cable (or clothesline) you'll need to suspend your hoop, a short review of the Pythagorean Theorem (you remember it, of course) is in order. It says: In a right triangle, the square of the measure of the hypotenuse equals the sum of the squares of the measures of two legs. Don't wring your hands in dismay: it's easier than it sounds.

Measure or generously estimate the height of the limb (a) from where you want to hang your hoop. Then decide where you will anchor your cable. Again, measure or generously estimate the distance from the base of the tree to where you will anchor the cable (b). Now locate your calculator. Plug the measurements into the following formula:

$a^2 + b^2 = c^2$. Check your calculations again. It's easier to measure twice and cut once. This is the length of steel cable you need to purchase.

2

Select a drill bit slightly smaller than the diameter of the nail or screw you have chosen. Drill a hole in the hoop. Insert the nail or screw in the hole and force it through. You will secure your candle on the nail or screw point.

3

Make a small loop at one end of the cable. Secure the loop around the hoop opposite your nail or screw. Fasten the loop with a ferrule and stop.

4

Repeat step 3 at the other end of the cable. Run the cable through the end of the snap link. Fasten the loop with a ferrule and stop.

5

Do you like to climb trees? If so, you can climb a ladder to loop the free end of the cable over the desired limb. If you have an aversion to heights, simply toss the free end of the cable over the limb.

6

Place a candle on the nail or screw point, light it, and hoist the hoop. You can secure the cable around the trunk of a small tree or to a stake firmly anchored in the ground. Leave the hoop suspended in the air after the candle burns down—it's a striking and unusual focal point for your outdoor space.

Bluebird of Happiness Lights

Designer
Terry Taylor

A flock of imaginary, night-flying bluebirds lives in these tin birdhouses. Can you picture the pale blue lights guiding the flock from their nighttime wanderings back to their homes in your garden?

Metal birdhouse ornaments

Light strand with candelabra bulb sockets

Several blue 4-watt light bulbs

Floral tape (optional)

Additional minilight strands (optional)

Pliers

Marking pen

Large nail or awl

Hammer

Tin snips

Half-round file

What You Do

1

Purchase as many birdhouse ornaments as you have light sockets on your strand. There are many varieties and sizes of birdhouse ornaments available in craft stores. If you can't find metal, try cardboard or wood. Just adapt the directions and tools to suit your material.

2

Remove the bottom of each birdhouse. Use the pliers to open the unsoldered seams holding the bottom to the sides of each ornament. If the bottoms of your ornaments are soldered on, use the tin snips to remove them.

3

Center a light socket on the roof of a birdhouse. Trace around the socket with the marking pen. Repeat for each house.

4

Punch small holes in the center of the marked circles using a large nail and the hammer.

5

Use the tip of the snips to enlarge the punched holes, then cut inside of the marked line. Don't cut too closely to the marked line. You don't want to cut the hole too large. You can enlarge the hole by filing it with the half-round file. File any sharp edges.

6

Place a socket on the roof of a birdhouse, reach inside holding the bulb, and screw the bulb into the socket. Repeat with each socket on the strand. You may want to alternate blue and white bulbs, or use all blue bulbs if you have enough.

7

You may wish to intersperse additional lights along the light strand. If so, wind a minilight strand around the strand. For a more finished appearance, wind floral tape tightly around the two light strands.

Moonlight Gardens:
Heavenly Scents and
Earthy Delights

The intoxicating scent of night-blooming flowers tempts you outdoors as the moon begins to rise. While color is the guiding principal of most gardens during the day, different intensities of white and silver dominate the night garden, and moon-loving plants shine with a luminous coating on their leaves. A moonlight garden is a delight to the senses—the white flowers and incandescent foliage captivate the eye, while the heady scent of night-blooming flowers sends us into olfactory bliss.

Here are a few examples of night-blooming and night-fragrant plants that can add enjoyment to your outdoor evenings.

Evening Primrose
Oenothera biennis

The yellow or soft white blossoms of this vine-climbing biannual open every evening in the summer and spread a lemony fragrance into the air. The evening primrose delights not only the eyes and nose, but also the ear—you can hear a small pop as the blossoms burst open at dusk.

Moonflowers
Ipomoea alba

A cousin of the morning glory, this vine-climbing plant features white trumpet-shaped flowers that open in slow motion every evening just at sunset. Their blooms begin to retreat just as the day breaks. Their sweet, strong smell is unmistakable, and they are considered a must for any moon garden.

Night Phlox or "Midnight Candy"
Zaluzianskyana capensis

The tiny flowers of this low-growing plant are tightly closed during the day and appear to be crimson on the outside. They open to a pure white blossom at dusk, releasing an almond-honey or vanilla-like fragrance into the air.

Angel's Trumpet
Datura arborea (Brugmansia)

Its long, white, trumpet-shaped flowers droop downward during the day, but at night, angel's trumpet blossoms point upward and emit a sweet scent. Variations of this flower can be found with yellow and red blossoms, but pure white is the best choice for a night garden (see photo).

Citronella Flower Power

Designer
Terry Taylor

Why settle for the standard-issue citronella candlepots when you can make these folksy tin flower containers in any size you wish? Make a tabletop bouquet from tiny evaporated milk cans, or plant citronella candle flowers of all sizes throughout your garden to light the night.

Tin cans

Heavy work gloves*

Can opener

Soap and water

Several sheets of copy paper

Cellophane tape

Pencil

Scissors

Permanent marker

Wire cutters

Tin snips

¾-inch (1.9 cm) dowel or broomstick, 4 inches (10.2 cm) long

*Wear heavy work gloves while cutting and rolling the tin.

What You Do

1
Remove the tops and paper labels from your cans. Clean the cans with warm soapy water, rinse, and dry them.

2
Wrap a sheet of copy paper around a can. If the can is taller or wider than a single sheet, tape another to the first one. Cut the paper to fit around the can, as if it were a label.

3
Fold the length of paper in half three times. Draw a curving petal shape or simple triangle about 2 inches (5.1 cm) tall at the top of one of the folds. Trim the excess from around the shape you just drew. Unfold the length of paper. This is your template for marking petals on the can.

4
Wrap and tape the template around the can. Trace the petal shapes with the marker. Remove the pattern and set it aside. If you're making several candles of the same size, you can use it again.

5
Use the wire cutters to cut the rim of the can at the top point of each petal. Don't use your tin snips to cut through the rim—you'll wear out the snips and eventually your cuts will be uneven. Trim each petal with tin snips following the marked pattern.

6
Holding the length of dowel in one hand, place it at the tip of a petal and use your thumbs to roll the petal over the dowel. Repeat this process for the rest of the petals.

7
Create as many tin flowers as desired following steps 1 through 6.

8
To complete your garden of citronella flowers, follow the basic container candle instructions on page 105.

Floating World Koi Pond Candles

Designer
Chris Rankin

Soothing water and lush vegetation make this unusual water feature a garden highlight. Don't loose sight of it at night—add floating candles to accentuate its serene beauty. If you don't have a koi pond, substitute with a water feature you create yourself.

What You Need

Water feature, such as a koi pond
Floating candles

What You Do

1

You can use any garden water feature for this project—from a swimming pool to a galvanized metal tub filled with water. Substitute colorful leaves or lush blossoms from your garden for the water lilies and parrot feather plants that grow in this charming old-fashioned laundry sink. If you are using a koi pond with living plants, trim excess vegetation before adding candles to prevent fire.

2

Choose floating candles to set the theme for your evening. Floating candles come in different colors and shapes from flower, fish, or star-shaped candles, to simple rounded candles such as those used in this project. Wax floats, but the trick is to get it to float upright. Typically, a candle that is wider than it is tall will float. You can use the instructions on page 105 to make your own floater candles in molds such as cupcake tins or small gelatin molds.

3

Floating candles usually burn for 2 to 4 hours. Keep an eye on your candles as they begin to burn down to make sure they don't ignite the lily pads or other floating plants. Make sure to remove the spent candles at the end of the evening so that your koi fish don't try to eat them!

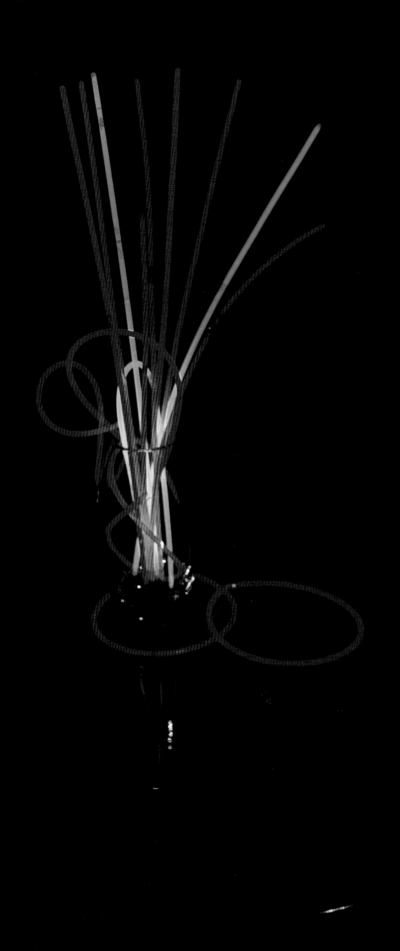

Technicolor Light Bouquet

Designer
Chris Rankin

Impress your guests with a sleek, chic centerpiece made from glowsticks. A spirited way to light up the night for revelry, these inexpensive lights come in many shapes, sizes, and colors.

What You Need

Commercial glowsticks*
Glass vase (optional)
Glass flower frog (optional)
Freezer

* Note: The long thin glowsticks used at amusement parks and fairs come with a clip on each end so that they can be shaped into circles or strung together. The shorter, thicker glowsticks found at camping supply stores don't have a mechanism for binding them together, but you can make holes in their end wrappings with a hole punch, and bind them together with string or wire.

What You Do

1

Wait until just before your event to start snapping the glowsticks and activating their chemicals. They will lose their glow over the course of a few hours, so you'll want them to be at their strongest just as guests are arriving.

2

Arrange your glowsticks artfully as an outdoor table centerpiece. Try placing a dozen glowsticks in a glass flower frog at the bottom of a vase to fashion a bright bouquet. Join the ends of glowsticks together to form circles or hoops to be wrapped around outdoor furniture, tree branches, or shrubbery. Link glowsticks together into a strand of multi-colored lights to be strung around the deck or patio. Set a table with glowstick napkin-rings for an illuminating and entertaining party favor.

3

Glowsticks will start to fade after about four hours. After your gathering ends, put your glowsticks in the freezer. The low temperature will refresh the chemicals so you can use them again at another event.

Glorious Glowsticks

It's hard to resist the allure of a glowstick. Kids at amusement parks aren't the only ones who are captivated by their glow. In recent years, grown-up party-goers have also fallen under their spell, lining up to buy them at rock concerts and laser shows. The luminous wands have been seen strung around the necks of revelers ringing in the new year from Times Square to Red Square. What makes the glowstick so irresistible? The colors are so impossibly brilliant that people find it hard to keep their eyes off them. The secret to their appeal is based in science that's both simple and complex.

What Makes Them Glow?

Many chemical reactions produce both light and heat: a burning candle is an example of this. Chemical reactions that produce light without heat produce "cool light" or *chemiluminescence*. An organic occurrence of this phenomenon is the firefly. A man-made example is the glowstick.

How Do Glowsticks Work?

A thin glass ampule inside the stick breaks when it's bent. This results in the mixing and reaction of two chemicals that cause an "excited" state inside the glowstick. The chemicals "relax" to their normal state by dumping their energy into a fluorescent dye molecule in the stick. The dye releases the energy as brilliantly colored light.

In labs, glowsticks are often used to show the effect of temperature on chemical reaction rates. All chemical reactions are slower at lower temperatures and faster at higher temperatures. Immersing a glowstick in a glass of warm water will intensify, but shorten, the stick's luminous activity. Conversely, chilling a glowstick will dull yet prolong the glow.

Stylish Tile Candleholder

Designer
Allison Smith

Discover the harmony of the elements in this easy-going and weather-worthy design that uses the back side of ceramic tiles. An ideal display for your bead and rock collections, this candleholder will brighten any outdoor setting.

What You Need

5 unglazed quarry tiles, each 6 x 6 inches (15.2 x 15.2 cm)

Quick-drying epoxy for ceramics

16-gauge copper wire, 4 yards (3.6 m) long

Large brass washer

Large brass wing nut

Assorted brass nuts, wing nuts, and bolts

Assorted ceramic beads

Sand

River stones or polished rocks

Candles

Plate for mixing epoxy

Epoxy brush

Rotary tool with grinder bit

Wire cutters

Pencil

What You Do

1

When you purchase the tiles, have one of them custom trimmed to use as the base tile. Cut the base tile so that the other four tiles, which will rest on top of it, fit together without overlapping. After your base tile has been cut, test to make sure the tiles will fit together to form a box, and make any adjustments.

2

Decide how you will position your side tiles before you mix the epoxy. Following the manufacturer's directions, mix enough epoxy to adhere one side tile at a time.

3

Apply a generous layer of epoxy along the bottom inside edge of your first side tile. Adhere this to your base tile. One edge of the tile will extend beyond the edge of the base tile. Hold the tile in place until set.

4

Starting with the extended edge, continue attaching side tiles. Apply epoxy to both the bottom and side seams. Remember to hold each side tile in place until it's set. Wait for the epoxy to completely dry. Use the rotary tool fitted with the grinder bit to remove the excess glue from the seams of your tile box.

5

Measure and cut four pieces of copper wire, each 1 yard (.9 m) long. Wrap one length of wire around the center of the tile box. Firmly twist the wire and let the ends dangle free. Repeat this step with all three remaining wires.

6

Gather the loose wire ends and thread them through the center of the large washer. Bend each wire back, over, and up through the washer one at a time. Collect the wire ends and thread them through the brass wing nut.

7

Thread the beads, wing nuts, bolts, and washers onto four wires you choose in any pattern you desire. Secure the beaded wires by twisting a very tight coil near the last bead. Individually coil the remaining wire ends around the pencil to form springs, or shape the wire in a circle to form spirals.

8

Fill your tile box with sand, and place the candle in the center. Arrange the river stones or polished rocks around the candle to complete your new outdoor lantern.

Vine Glorious Lights

Designer
Dyan Mai Peterson

Adorn your tree branches, trellis, arbor, or latticework with this night-blooming vine—a strand of minilights covered with ornamental gourds. These lights shine with a subtle beauty, enhancing the design of your garden features.

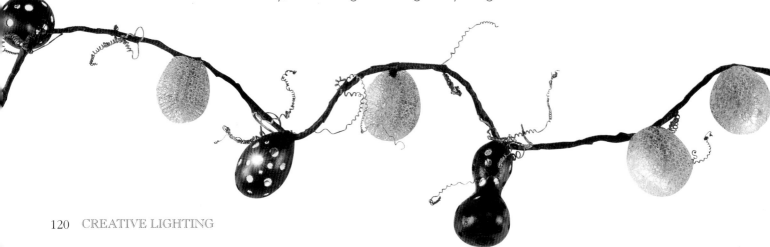

Small, ornamental gourds

Small, Mexican luffa gourds (*L. Operculata*)

Basin with water

Metal kitchen scrub pad

Clear spray lacquer or clear acrylic varnish

Brown floral tape

Floral wire

Minilight strand

Curly paper "tendrils" *

Pencil

Sharp kitchen knife with serrated blade

Keyhole or hobby saw

Power drill with assorted drill bits, 1/32 to 7/16 inch (1 mm to 1.1 cm)

available in the floral or paper section of a craft-supply store

What You Do

1

Soak the small ornamental gourds in warm water for up to 15 minutes, then scrub off any mold and dirt with the metal scrub pad. Allow the gourds to dry.

2

Estimate the diameter of a light bulb and socket on the minilight strand. Select a drill bit that is the same or a slightly larger size than the diameter of the bulb and socket. Use the power drill to make a hole at the top of each ornamental gourd. Insert a light bulb and socket to check the fit.

3

Using the 1/32-inch (1 mm) drill bit, drill a hole on either side of the hole you drilled in step 2.

4

Use a variety of drill bit sizes to drill additional holes in the gourd. The number of holes you create will determine the amount of light the gourd emits. Shake out the small seeds from the gourds. Save them for next year's crop.

5

Spray the drilled ornamental gourds with lacquer or acrylic varnish. Allow them to dry.

6

Crack the thin shells of the luffa gourds and peel them to expose the fibrous interior. Set them aside.

7

Starting at the plug end of the light strand, wrap the strand with the brown floral tape. Stop wrapping just before the first light socket.

8

Thread a short length of floral wire through the tiny holes at the top of each gourd. Insert a bulb and socket in the top hole of each gourd. Secure the gourd to the strand, twisting the ends of the floral wire together. Continue wrapping the strand with floral tape. Using floral tape, cover the twisted ends of wire, and then attach paper tendrils at intervals along the length of the strand.

9

Slip the luffa gourds over the light bulbs along the strand. Alternate luffa gourds and the drilled ornamental gourds along the light strand as desired.

Backyard Fire Pit

Designer
Chris Rankin

As the evening chill sets in and the stars begin to twinkle up above, a blazing fire in your own backyard fire pit beckons you to sit and stay a while. Spend a few hours with friends telling stories or singing songs, enjoying the company, and the warmth and mystery of the fire.

What You Need

3 cups (600 g) of flour

12 to 15 large stones

25 small stones (each should fit in the palm of your hand)

Gravel, 1 wheelbarrow load

Dry-washed sand, 20-pound (9072 g) bag

Spade

Hoe

Rounded digging shovel

Metal rake

Split logs

Kindling

What You Do

1

Survey your backyard for a location for your fire pit. Choose a spot at least 30 feet (9.1 m) away from the nearest plants, trees, or other vegetation. Make sure there are no roots or overhanging branches in the area that could catch fire.

2

Using a spade or hoe, dig a circle about 10 feet (3 m) in diameter, clearing the area of grass and roots. Your circle doesn't have to be deep, but you should make sure there are no roots underneath the area.

3

In the center of the circle, use flour to create another circle about 3 feet (91.4 cm) across. The fire will be contained in the center of this inner circle.

4

Create another flour circle 3-½ (1.06 m) feet outside the inner circle you just created. This outer circle will be a buffer zone for containing the fire.

5

Dig out the inner circle using your shovel. Your hole should be at least 1 foot (30.5 cm) deep, but no more than 5 feet (1.5 m) deep.

6

Put the small rocks into the hole as a liner. These allow you to remove the ashes without removing soil, and help to contain the fire within the inner circle.

7

Place the large stones around the outter edge of the hole as a border. Put them as close together as possible. Dig small ruts to secure them into position if necessary.

8

For greater safety, spread a layer of gravel 3 to 4 inches (7.6 cm to 10.2 cm) thick around the fire ring.

9

Arrange the split logs in the fire pit. Use kindling to get the fire started, and don't forget the marshmallows!

Vellum Stamped Minilight Shades
(page 94)

Flourless Cake Pan Sconces
(page 86)

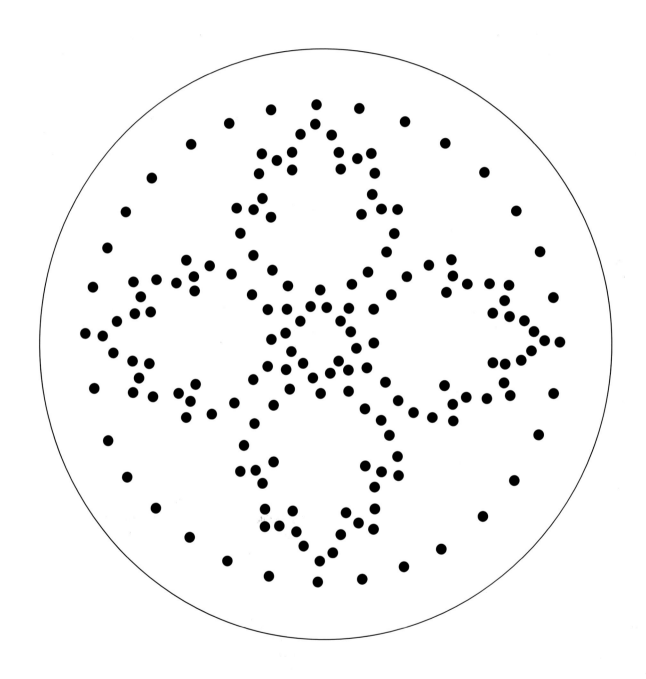

Designers

Chris Bryant, an art director at Lark Books, is the ingenious co-creator of *The New Book of Table Settings* (Lark, 2000).

Robin Clark owns Robin's Wood, Ltd., where he manufactures outdoor products for people and wildlife. In his off-hours he enjoys trying his hand at other woodworking projects.

Sheila Ennis is a writer and artist living in Boston, Massachusetts. She has a thriving small business specializing in decorative paint finishes.

Susan Kieffer traded the sand, sun, and fun of Key West for the Blue Ridge mountains of Asheville, North Carolina. Her resume runs the gamut from catalog buyer to television camerawoman to clothing designer. She works for *Folkwear Patterns* and *Fiberarts* magazine.

Diana Light is an accomplished artisan who specializes in one-of-a-kind painted and etched glass pieces. Visit her website at www.angelfire.com/NCZ/diana/bluelight.html.

Anne McCloskey lives in Copley, Ohio. She enjoys changing old, flea market items into wonderful new designs.

Jean Tomaso Moore has been creating art—in one form or another—for as long as she can remember. She lives with her humble, patient husband, Richard, in the beautiful mountains of Asheville, North Carolina.

Dyan Mai Peterson is a nationally known gourd artist. She enjoys experimenting with any size or shape of gourd that she can find or grow. She creates decorative bowls, jewelry, dolls, and more in her studio in Asheville, North Carolina.

Rob Pulleyn, guiding light of Lark Books, usually is a very hands-off manager. But when the spirit moves him, he can't help using his hands to whip up projects for our books. He lives in Wise Acres, North Carolina.

Chris Rankin is a multi-talented designer and the author of several books, including *Splendid Samplers* (Sterling/Lark, 1995).

Allison Smith lives in Asheville, North Carolina. Her home-based business specializes in providing deluxe tourist accommodations in remote locations around the world. She is an avid crafter and designer, in addition to being a full-time mother. You can reach her at waterrockgarden@hotmail.com.

Cathy Smith is an artist working in a wide variety of media. She lives in western North Carolina with her husband, son, and assorted feline, canine, and reptilian family members.

Heather Smith, assistant editor at Lark Books, grew up on the coast of Maine, where she was an environmental educator. She now enjoys biking and hiking in the mountains of western North Carolina.

Murray Spencer gardens in western North Carolina.

Nicole Tuggle combines bookbinding techniques with her passion for mail art to create unique letters, fine art, and gift items. Visit her website at www.sigilation.com.

Terry Taylor is an artist and designer. He lives on the west bank of the French Broad River with his horticulturally inclined partner, Jeff Webb.

Sherri Hunter Warner is a sculptor of large-scale concrete and mosaic public works. Her work can be seen at the Nashville International Airport and the Memphis/Shelby County Public Library. She is the author of *Creating with Concrete*, a Lark book on concrete projects for the garden. She lives in Bell Buckle, Tennessee with her husband, Martin.

Acknowledgments

We would like to thank Frank and Sherry Taylor, Lee and Alice Johnson, Michael and Kathy Evans, Heather Spencer and Charles Murray, and Jeffrey Webb for their patience and generous use of both homes and gardens for photography locations. Thank you to J. Dabney Peeples Design Associates, Inc. of Easley, South Carolina for their assistance in finding locations.

Additional photographs for this book were provided by Chiminea Express of Blowing Rock, North Carolina (www.finaltouches.com) (page 89), Richard Hasselberg of Asheville, North Carolina (page 6), David Graham (page 11, top photo), Epifanio Juarez of Juarez Design, Palo Alto, California (bottom photo, page 9), Signe Nielsen (page 11, bottom photo), Nightscaping of Redlands, California (page 9, top photo, page 10, page 12).

Index